© Aladdin Books Ltd 1988

All rights reserved

Designed and produced by
Aladdin Books Ltd
70 Old Compton Street
London W1

Design   David West
              Children's Book Design
Editorial Planning   Clark Robinson Limited
Editor   Bibby Whittaker
Researcher   Cecilia Weston-Baker
Illustrated by   Ron Hayward Associates
              and Aziz A. Khan

EDITORIAL PANEL
The author, Linda Gamlin, has degrees in Biochemistry and Applied Biology, and has contributed to several encyclopedias.

The educational consultant, Peter Thwaites, is Head of Geography at Windlesham House School in Sussex.

The editorial consultant, John Clark, has contributed to many information and reference books.

First published in the
United States in 1988 by
Gloucester Press
387 Park Avenue South
New York, NY 10016

ISBN 0-531-17118-3

Library of Congress Catalog
Card Number: 88-50506

Printed in Belgium

TODAY'S WORLD

THE HUMAN RACE

LINDA GAMLIN

GLOUCESTER PRESS
New York · London · Toronto · Sydney

CONTENTS

STUDYING THE PAST	4
WALKING UPRIGHT	6
MAKING TOOLS	8
THE HAND-AXE MAKER	10
MODERN HUMANS	12
THE DAWN OF CIVILIZATION	**14**
AGRICULTURE AND CITIES	16
THE RISE OF CIVILIZATION	18
EXPLORATION AND COLONIZATION	20
PEOPLES OF THE WORLD	**22**
HUMAN LANGUAGE	24
RELIGIONS AND CUSTOMS	26
THE THIRD WORLD	28
THE INDUSTRIAL AGE	30
THE HIGH-TECH AGE	32
HUMAN EVOLUTIONARY TREE	**34**
GLOSSARY/INDEX	**35/36**

The front cover photograph shows children of various races and national origins.

INTRODUCTION

Throughout the world today, there are people of many different races, with skins of different colors. But as well as such physical differences, there are variations in languages, social customs and living conditions which also divide the human race. It is all too easy to misunderstand the attitudes of people who have a different culture or religion, and this is unfortunately one cause of many of the world's present problems.

Scientists who study the origins of humankind have much to tell us about ourselves. They know that we originated in Africa more than 5 million years ago, and that all human beings are descended from one common ancestral race. Biological studies tell the same story. Comparisons of the molecules that make up our bodies show that we are all remarkably similar under the skin. Most racial differences are adaptations to different climates, which have evolved as humankind gradually spread to each habitable part of the world. But as science shows, we are all members of the same race – the human race.

Early humans evolved on the plains of Africa.

STUDYING THE PAST

The past is divided into two main eras: the prehistoric and the historic. History began between 4,500 and 5,000 years ago, when writing was first used to record events. Little information was recorded at first, but in time the historical records became more detailed. Information about prehistoric times is more difficult to obtain – the main evidence is what we can dig up out of the ground. Even in studies of historic times, a lot of useful information can come from such archaeological digs.

The earliest human ancestors were ape-like animals, and the only remains they left behind were their teeth and bones, which sometimes turned to fossils. The study of fossils – animal or human – is known as paleontology.

In time, our ancestors began to make tools out of sticks, and then out of pebbles. Stone tools were very durable and they have survived more often than bones. Other human activities, such as building huts and making fires, also left evidence behind.

Over the centuries, human activities became more and more complicated, and with each stage there is more evidence to find – complex stone tools appear, then stone carvings and cave paintings, then buildings, pottery and metal tools. The study of such man-made objects is called archaeology.

Teeth
Teeth are harder than bones and they are often the only part of the body to be preserved. An electron microscope can reveal how fragments of bone leave a particular type of scratch mark, showing that meat was on the menu. Soil particles from tubers and roots leave a deeper type of scratch mark.

Footprints
Very occasionally footprints are preserved in mud or volcanic ash, if it dries to a hard surface and is then covered by more sediment.

Bones
Bones eventually rot, but where they are preserved by sediment, they may turn into fossils. In this process, minerals from the rock gradually replace the bone itself, creating a stone 'replica' of the bone.

Plants
Plants produce pollen grains which have a characteristic shape and pattern for each species of plant. They are also very tough and are often preserved. They can be seen in rocks using a microscope, and can reveal what the climate was like at the time, and what sort of food plants our ancestors ate.

Dating a site

Finding out the age of a site is very important. One method of dating is based on radioactive materials, which occur naturally and "decay" at a fixed rate. A radioactive form of carbon, carbon-14, is found in the carbon dioxide gas in the atmosphere, and therefore in all living plants and animals. Once they die, no more carbon is taken into the body, and the carbon-14 already present slowly decays. By measuring the amount remaining, scientists can work out how long ago organisms died. Carbon dating works well, but only for objects less than 70,000 years old.

Older archaeological sites are more difficult, but the ages of some can be worked out using potassium-argon dating, which measures the radiation from a radioactive form of potassium found in volcanic ash.

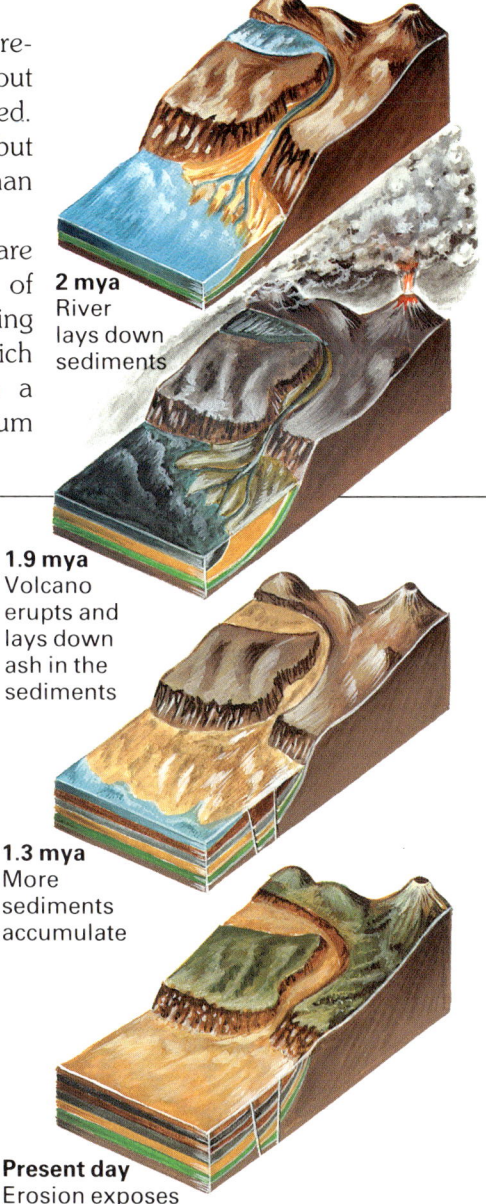

2 mya River lays down sediments

1.9 mya Volcano erupts and lays down ash in the sediments

1.3 mya More sediments accumulate

Present day Erosion exposes sediments

mya = million years ago

Wood and hide
Although wooden tools and animal hides are not preserved on prehistoric sites such as this, they would survive on more recent sites.

Fire
Fire leaves burned stones and baked clay, although it is not always easy to tell if the fire was a natural one or a man-made campfire. In later sites the signs are clearer, because people built hearths and used them often.

Tools
In prehistoric sites, any wooden tools have long since rotted away, but stone tools are often preserved. The way in which the tool is used leaves a particular "polish" on its surface. By looking at this tool under a microscope scientists would know that it had been used to scrape animal skins – which shows that skins were used for making bags, tents or clothing.

Studying our past requires a lot of detective work – especially on prehistoric sites such as this one, dating from half a million years ago. Archaeologists must be able to piece together fragments of evidence to build up a picture of how our ancestors lived.

As well as human bones, the remains of animals which were eaten are often found at campsites. They show if the people hunted big game or small. Cut marks on the bones from stone tools reveal how the animal was butchered.

Once people began burying their dead, far more human bones were preserved.

WALKING UPRIGHT

> Hominid is the name given to all human-like creatures, including living humans and extinct forms. Not all of these were our direct ancestors.
>
> Lucy was about 20 years old when she died. Although this seems young to us, she was probably middle-aged or even old for a hominid.

Human beings belong to a group of mammals known as primates, most of which live in trees. Our nearest relatives, the apes, have a special way of moving through the trees, swinging by their arms from branch to branch. This form of movement requires a very flexible type of shoulder joint, known as a ball-and-socket joint. We have this type of shoulder joint, and it can be seen in action when a tennis player serves. Our flexible shoulders show that we once swung from branch to branch – before we eventually took to walking upright.

A fossil called Lucy

The oldest hominid fossils are 3.75 million years old, and come from a region in Ethiopia known as the Afar Triangle. One female skeleton was nicknamed Lucy by the American paleontologist who discovered her. Lucy was a very special find because over 40 per cent of her skeleton was preserved – an unusually large amount. The shape of her leg- and hip-bones shows that Lucy walked upright. But her toe-bones have a slight curve to them, suggesting that treeclimbing was still important. These early hominids may have spent the day on the ground searching for food, and climbed up into the trees at night (as baboons do) to be safe from lions and other predators.

By comparing DNA and proteins from our bodies with those from chimpanzees and gorillas, scientists can tell roughly how long ago we took a separate evolutionary path from the apes. They think this happened 5-10 million years ago. Unfortunately there are no fossils from this period to show us what the very earliest hominids – Lucy's ancestors – looked like.

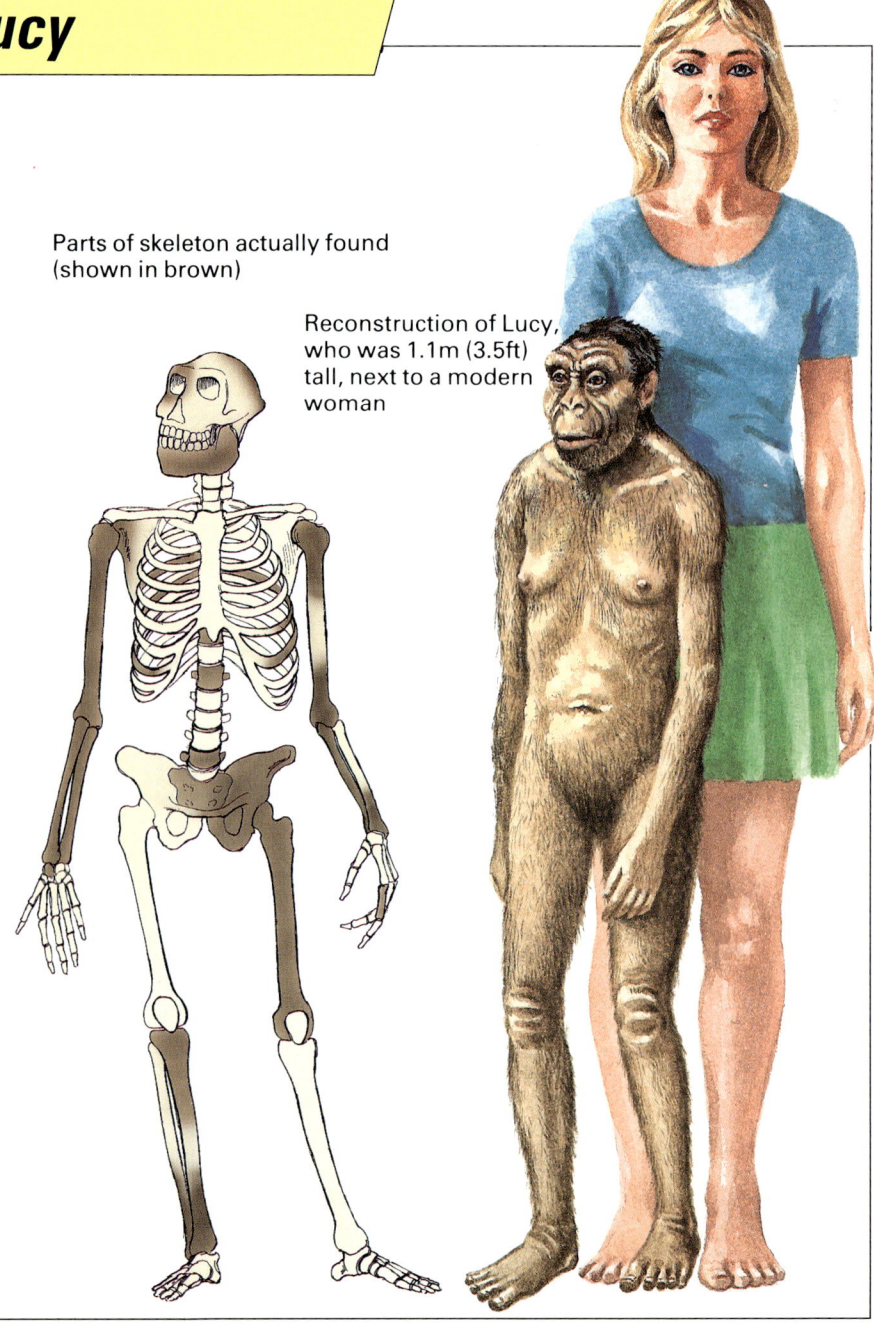

Parts of skeleton actually found (shown in brown)

Reconstruction of Lucy, who was 1.1m (3.5ft) tall, next to a modern woman

Fossil footprints

Fossil footprints, found in Tanzania, confirm that hominids like Lucy walked upright. A volcanic eruption covered the ground with ash 3.75 million years ago. When three hominids then walked across the ash, they left their prints for all time, because the ash hardened and set.

Upright walking has changed our hands and feet. In an ape both are adapted for gripping branches – so they look much the same. In humans the feet are longer and narrower, to allow us to run fast, and the big toe is shorter because it has no need to grip. Because the hands are not used for movement they are free to perform other tasks. The thumb and fingers have both become longer to make the hands more skillful.

Fossil footprints

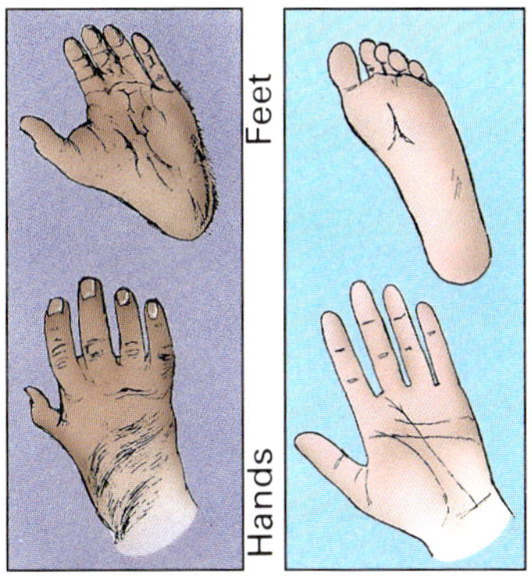

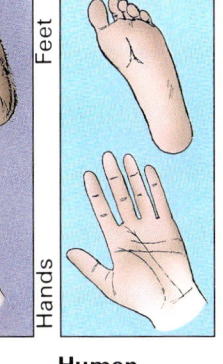
Gorilla

Human

Feet

Hands

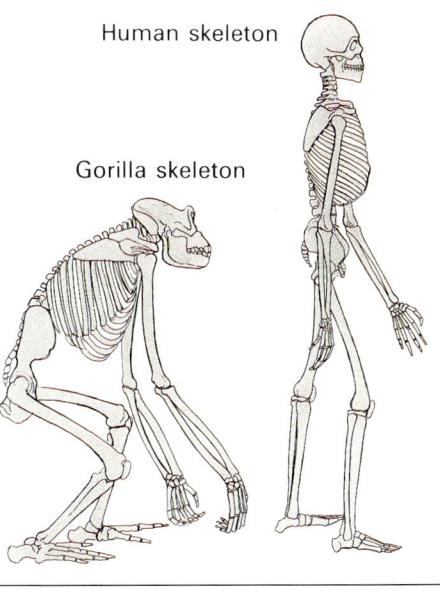
Human skeleton

Gorilla skeleton

The Australopithecines

Lucy and her fellow hominids are known to paleontologists as *Australopithecus afarensis*. *Australopithecus* is the name given to the earliest hominids, and to some later ones that were not our direct ancestors.

Two different types of australopithecines were living in Africa after hominids like Lucy had died out. One group, the robust australopithecines, or *Australopithecus robustus*, were large and heavily built – at least the males were. The females were probably much smaller. Despite their size, robust australopithecines appear to have been harmless plant-eaters. The microscopic scratches on their teeth show that they ate fruit, leaves and perhaps a few roots. They had small brains and it is unlikely that they made stone tools.

The gracile australopithecines were smaller and more lightly built, but they too had small brains. A few palaeontologists think that they were an off-shoot of the evolutionary line that led to man, as the robust australopithecines were. Most believe that they were our direct ancestors.

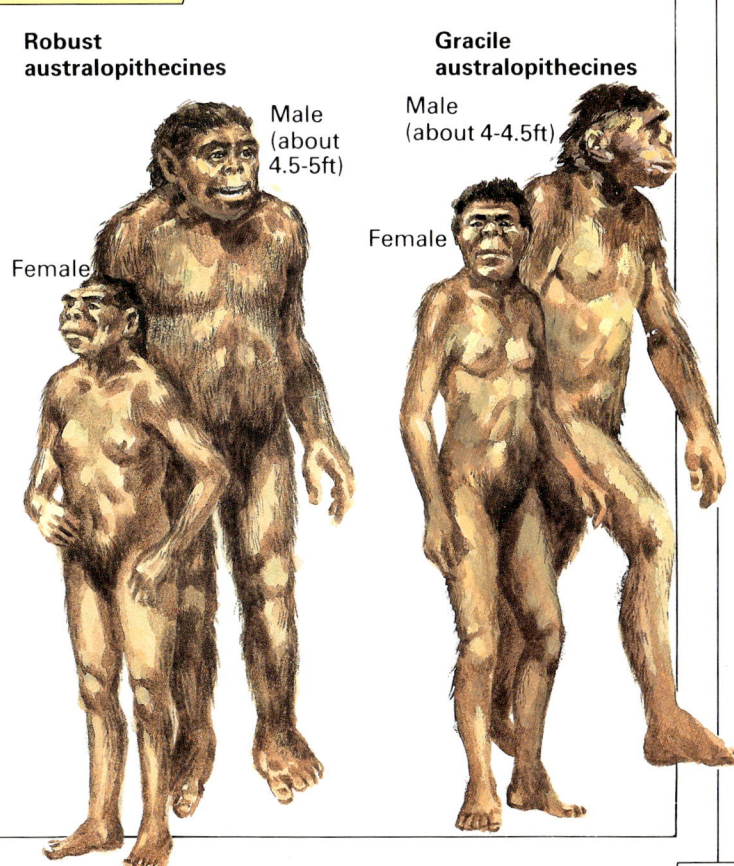

Robust australopithecines
Male (about 4.5-5ft)
Female

Gracile australopithecines
Male (about 4-4.5ft)
Female

MAKING TOOLS

Hominids that are thought to have been our direct ancestors are placed in the genus *Homo* – the same group as ourselves. The oldest stone tools for which archaeologists can be certain about the date come from the Omo Valley in southern Ethiopia. They are 2 – 2.2 million years old.

When paleontologists find a fossil skull, they can measure its volume to discover how large the brain was. Looking at fossil skulls from Africa, they find that the brain size gradually increases as time goes by. The first noticeable increase in size comes about 2 million years ago, and the hominids with the larger brains also have slightly flatter, less ape-like faces. They are called *Homo habilis* and it is thought that they were probably the first hominids to make stone tools, because tools began to appear in the fossil record at about the same time.

Finding tools

As the hominids' brain size increased they must have shown their greater intelligence in many different ways. They may have begun to talk, share food, and cooperate more with each other. But changes of this sort do not leave any trace in the fossil record. The main evidence we can find is that they began to make stone tools.

By looking at modern Athapaskan Indians of North America, we find that although stone is important to them, they also make use of wood, animal hide, and other materials that rot away. The tools of *Homo habilis* would have been much more primitive than these, but the point is the same: most of them would not have been preserved.

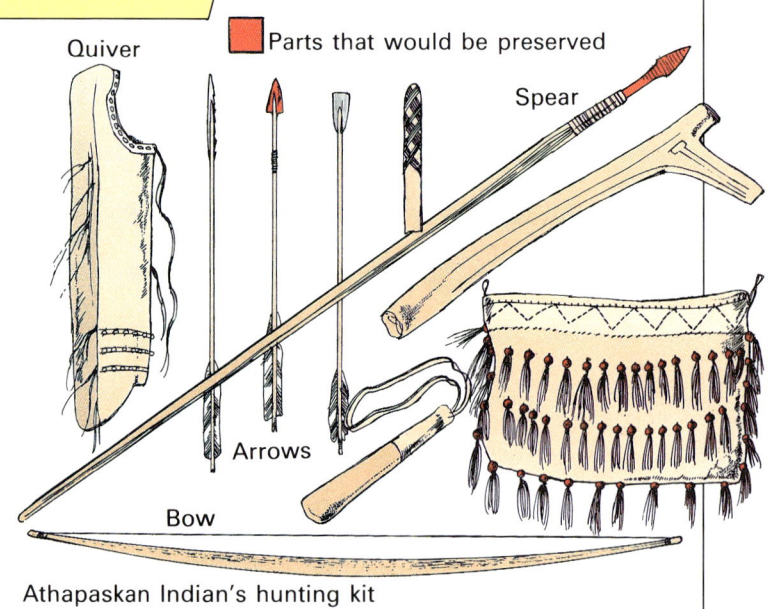

Athapaskan Indian's hunting kit

How stone tools were made

Making stone tools is not easy, and only certain types of stone will give a good result. By learning to make tools for themselves, modern archaeologists have discovered a great deal about our ancestors' skills. Having first chosen their stone, they struck it with a hammerstone at the correct angle to remove a flake. By removing more and more flakes, a chopper with a long cutting edge, as sharp as a steel knife, could be produced. The flakes themselves had sharp edges and could be held between finger and thumb and used for cutting meat or sharpening a stick.

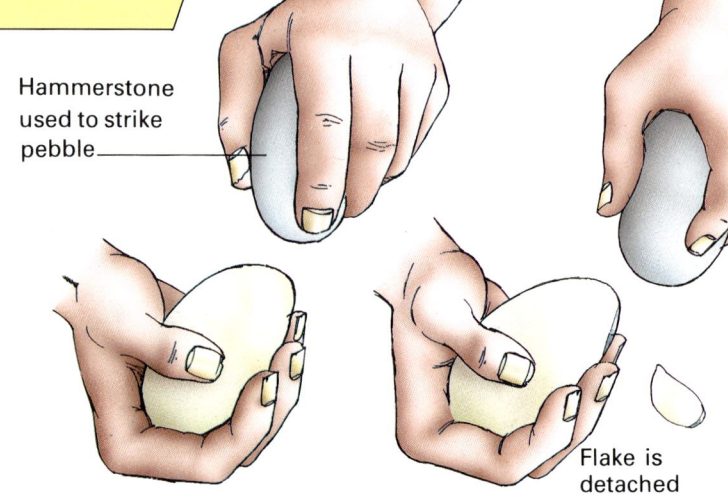

8

Handyman

Homo habilis means 'handyman' or 'skillful man' and refers to this hominid's ability to make stone tools. The type of stone used for most of the early tools is lava, which does not take a 'polish' in the same way that harder stone such as flint does. So microscope studies cannot reveal what these simple tools were used for. But they are often found together with bones, often those of large animals. At one site in Kenya, stone tools have been found with the remains of a hippopotamus. It seems unlikely that a group of *Homo habilis* hunters could have killed a hippo, so they were probably scavengers rather than hunters. They would have taken meat from animals that were already dead, as vultures do.

A skull of *Homo habilis*, the tool-maker

Homo habilis

Cutting up dead animal with stone tools

Collecting berries and other plant foods

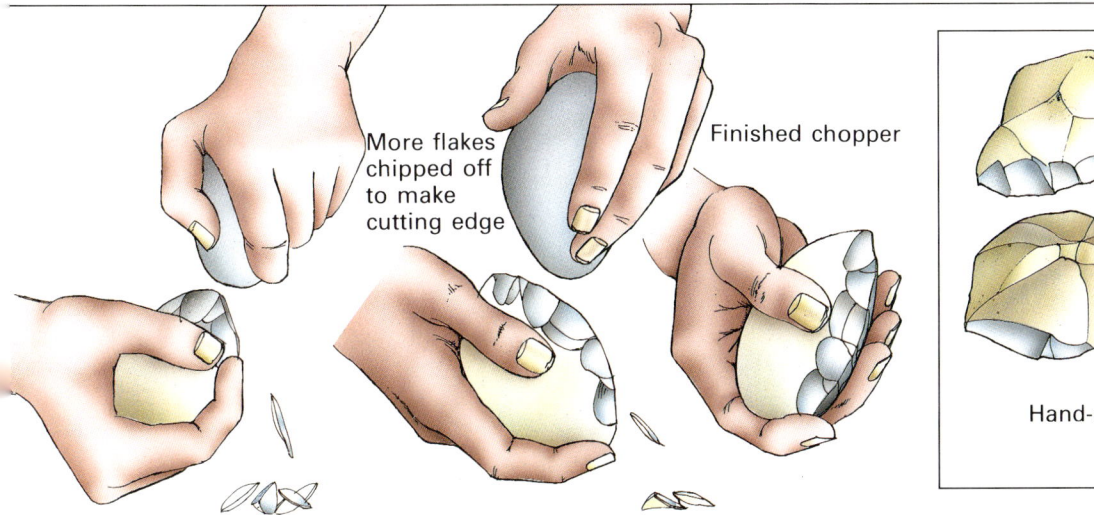

More flakes chipped off to make cutting edge

Finished chopper

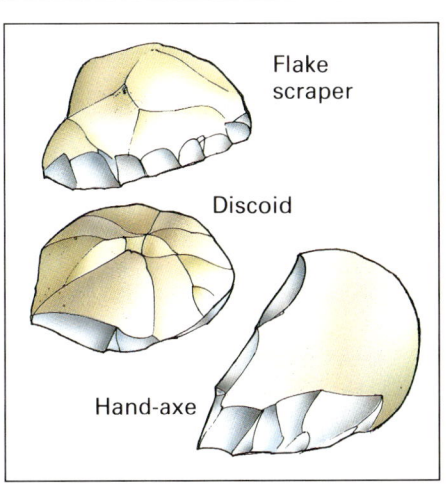

Flake scraper

Discoid

Hand-axe

THE HAND-AXE MAKER

Homo erectus lived for over a million years, and was the first hominid to hunt large game and use fire.
Taking over from *Homo habilis* fossils 1.5 million years ago, *erectus* continued until 200,000 years ago when forms transitional between *erectus* and *sapiens* appeared.

Rocks from East Africa which are 1.5 million years old show that by this time a new type of hominid had evolved from *Homo habilis*. Known as *Homo erectus*, this new hominid had the same sort of body as its *habilis* ancestors, but the skull was different. It had a larger braincase and heavy ridges of bone above the eyes – called brow-ridges. *Homo erectus* perfected the type of tool known as a hand-axe, and continued to use it for over a million years. This very successful hominid was the direct ancestor of our own human species, *Homo sapiens*.

Hunting big game

From scavenging on carcasses, *Homo erectus* probably moved on to hunting small game such as hares and bush-pigs. In time, the hunting skills of *Homo erectus* improved, and these more intelligent hominids began to go after bigger game. This required greater cooperation between the hominids, who must have hunted together in fairly large bands. One site in Kenya, known as Olorgessaillie, shows that they hunted giant baboons: huge quantities of baboon bones have been found, together with over 10,000 hand-axes. By watching how the local people hunt baboons today, it is possible to imagine the scene at Olorgessaillie, half a million years ago.

This was not the only way in which the diet of the *Homo erectus* hominids changed. Deep pits in their tooth enamel, produced by grit particles from soil, show that they were eating roots and tubers. In arid parts of Africa, where bush fires are common, many plants have huge underground storage roots. *Homo erectus* had obviously discovered this bountiful food supply.

1. At dusk, baboons gather in trees for the night. Hominids frighten them out of the trees by shouting and throwing stones.

3. Female baboons and young killed by other hunters and butchered nearby.

2. Group of hunters keep the large male baboons at bay.

Homo erectus

Out of Africa

Simple pebble tools from Pakistan and China suggest that *Homo habilis* left Africa as long as 1.8 million years ago. But these early migrations probably involved just a few scattered groups. *Homo erectus* hominids moved out of Africa in far greater numbers, and colonized much of Europe and Asia. There were probably successive waves of migrants, with the new arrivals mixing in with the older populations. Although the separate populations evolved in their own ways, the influx of new immigrants meant that they remained part of the same gene pool, so that *Homo erectus* in China, Spain or Africa continued to evolve in much the same direction.

Archaeologist excavating in a Spanish cave

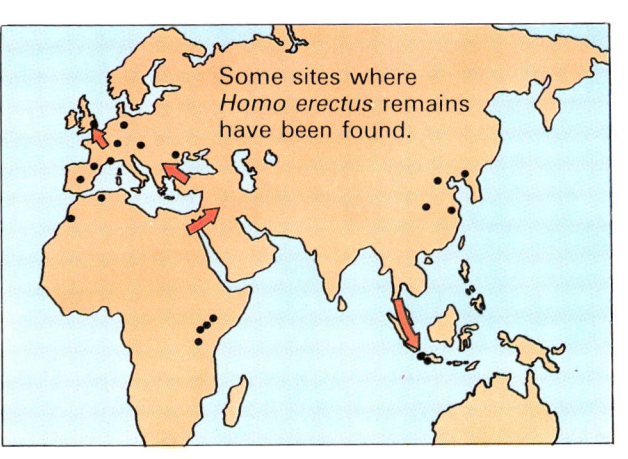

Some sites where *Homo erectus* remains have been found.

Hand-axes

Hand-axes have a blunt, rounded end that sits in the hand, and two sharp edges meeting in a point. They were sturdy cutting tools used mainly for jointing carcasses and cutting up the meat. Simple hand-axes were already made by *Homo habilis*, but as *Homo erectus* evolved, the hand-axe became larger and sharper. It was the characteristic tool of most *Homo erectus* groups, except those in China. Other tools, such as flakes and choppers, were still used.

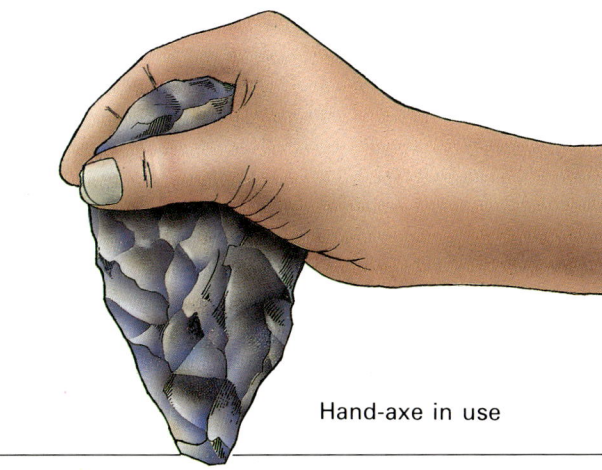

Hand-axe in use

Bigger brains

Australopithicus afarensis – Lucy and her relatives – had a brain size of 24 cubic inches. The brains of the robust australopithecines stayed about the same size, whereas those of the *Homo* line increased.

Homo habilis was probably a descendent of *afarensis*, but had a much larger brain, almost 49 cu. in. In early *Homo erectus* this rose to 55 cu. in., and increased to 67 cu. in. in later *erectus*. Our average brain size is now 82 cu. in.

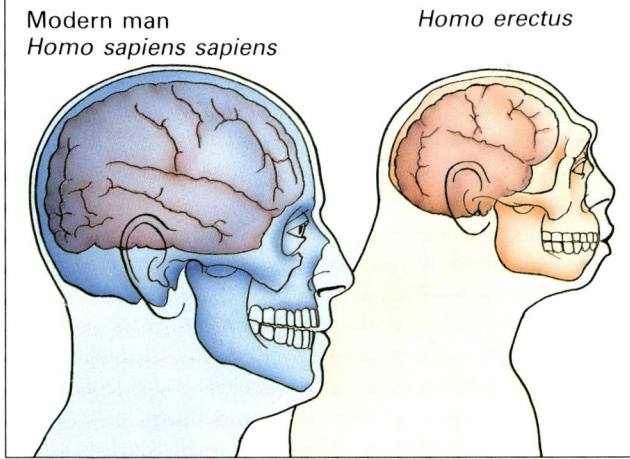

Modern man
Homo sapiens sapiens

Homo erectus

MODERN HUMANS

Our own species, *Homo sapiens*, first evolved from *Homo erectus* 300,000-200,000 years ago. Neanderthals, *Homo sapiens neanderthalensis*, lived from about 100,000 to 35,000 years ago. Fully modern man, *Homo sapiens sapiens* appeared about 40,000 years ago.

Most paleontologists agree that *Homo habilis* and *Homo erectus* had African origins. With *Homo sapiens*, however, the picture is not clear. Fossil skulls that are intermediate between *erectus* and *sapiens* are found in Africa, Asia and Europe, so it is difficult to say in which part of the world *sapiens* originated. One piece of evidence suggests that different *erectus* populations may have evolved towards the *sapiens* form at the same time: *erectus* teeth from China have an unusual feature seen also in modern Chinese and other Mongoloid people.

The Neanderthals

The Neanderthals were a type of *Homo sapiens* found in Europe and western Asia during part of the last Ice Age. They were thickset, muscular people, much stronger than we are, and probably just as intelligent. Their brains were actually slightly larger than ours, but they still had a long, low skull and heavy brow-ridges.

Neanderthals lived during one of the coldest parts of the Ice Age, and some of their features may have been adaptations to intense cold. They probably chewed hides to soften them for clothing and shoes – this is something that Eskimos do – and marks on Neanderthal teeth suggest that they did the same. The shape of the skull and face may have been partly due to the massive chewing muscles needed for this task.

There were several different groups of Neanderthals in different parts of Europe. One group, living in eastern Europe, specialized in hunting mammoths. Few trees grew in the bleak landscape they inhabited, so wood was in short supply. Mammoth bones made a good substitute and these people built their huts out of long bones.

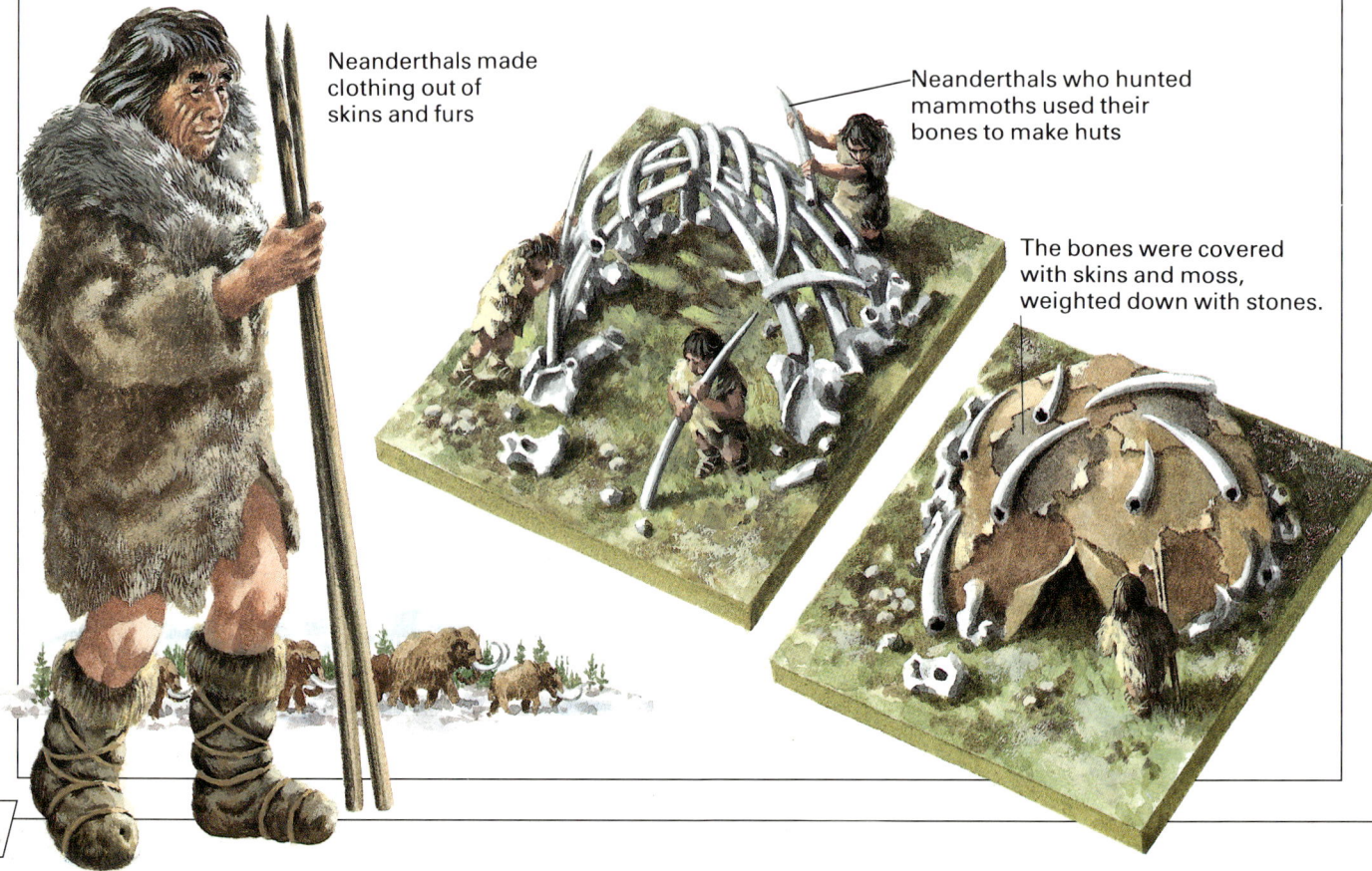

Neanderthals made clothing out of skins and furs

Neanderthals who hunted mammoths used their bones to make huts

The bones were covered with skins and moss, weighted down with stones.

Fully modern man

The group to which we belong is *Homo sapiens sapiens* – fully modern man. Nobody knows exactly where this group originated, but they gradually took over from other forms of *Homo sapiens*, including the Neanderthals.

The world was still in the grip of the last Ice Age when these modern people appeared. In Europe, their remains are concentrated in southern France, Spain and Italy, because the areas farther north were too cold and barren. Their main source of food was the reindeer, which is now found much farther north, in Scandinavia. Reindeer are migratory and the people probably followed the herds on their wanderings. Because of some unusual portraits – or caricatures as they appear to be – that are etched on the wall of a cave in France, we have an idea of what these people looked like.

La Marche cave portraits – about 40,000 years old

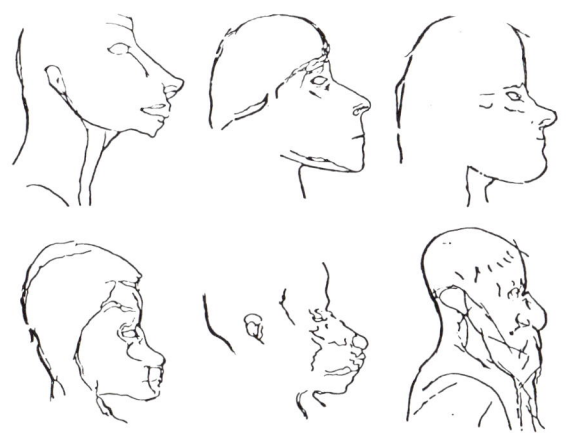

Reindeer provide materials for nomadic peoples.

Better tools

The tools made by *Homo sapiens sapiens* were far more varied and specialized than anything that had been seen before. They included needles made of bone or antler for sewing leather clothing. A stone tool called a burin was used to make the eye of the needle.

Necklaces and beads, for decorating clothing, were made from shell and bone. To drill holes in them, a sharp flint point attached to a wooden stick was used. The end of the stick fitted into a circular slot in a mouthpiece made of bone. By pushing a bow back and forth, the stick was made to rotate, thus drilling the hole.

Bone spear straightener

Flint knife with bone or wood handle

Flint sawing tool

Flint burin for boring holes

Serrated flint tool

Wood-and-bone drill in use

THE DAWN OF CIVILIZATION

About 200 caves and rock shelters, decorated by man during the Ice Age, have been found in southern France and northern Spain. The 'Age of Art' lasted from about 35,000 years ago until 10,000 years ago, when the last Ice Age ended. The famous cave of Lascaux was painted at the height of the period, about 15,000 years ago. Rock paintings in Tanzania date from 35,000 years ago, and may be the oldest in the world.

Up until 35,000 years ago, we have plenty of evidence about how humans found their food, made tools and built shelters. But we know almost nothing about what they were thinking. The first evidence of this sort appears with small carvings of animals found in Europe, and dramatic rock paintings found in Tanzania in Africa. These mark the beginning of the Age of Art.

The art of Europe and that of Africa were very different. The African rock paintings show both animals and humans, and are drawn in a striking, angular style. Most show some event, such as a hunt, or a quarrel between two groups of people. European cave paintings are much more difficult to understand, because they rarely show anything actually happening. They mainly show animals, drawn with beautiful flowing lines.

Magic and mystery

Apart from the 'cartoon' portraits from La Marche, humans are rarely shown in European cave art. But a few caves have pictures of strange figures, half man and half animal. These may represent shamans or witch doctors, people who were believed to have magic powers. Shamans are still found in many tribal societies in Africa and South America. The shaman may have worn the head and skin of an animal during magic ceremonies, so that he appeared half-animal, as in the paintings.

The mind of early man

There are several puzzling things about the cave art of Europe. The paintings were mostly in special caves that were not used for living in. Many different kinds of animals were shown, particularly bulls, horses and bison. But the bones left in the living caves show that the most important animals for food were reindeer – which very rarely appear in the paintings. This suggests that the paintings had some significance. The fact that these people buried some of their dead, and placed offerings in their graves, suggests that they may have believed in life after death.

An elaborate Stone Age burial chamber

The dawn of art

To make their paintings, these early people used special types of earth, found only in certain places, which have a natural strong color. The colors of these earths were red, yellow, black and brown. They mixed the earth with water to make paint and applied it with their fingers, or with a brush. They could have made a brush by fraying the end of a twig, or by binding stiff animal hairs to a stick – just like a modern-day paint brush. Sometimes they covered the wall of the cave with a thin layer of clay before they started work. Because most of the painted caves were deep underground, they had to work by the flickering light of lamps that burned animal fat.

15

AGRICULTURE AND CITIES

Agriculture began in the Near East between 12,000 and 10,000 years ago. It began independently in at least three other places: China, growing rice, over 7,000 years ago; Southeast Asia, growing yams, about 9,000 years ago; and Central America, with corn, about 7,000 years ago.

Life changed dramatically for early people when the Ice Age came to an end, although it was a change that took several thousand years to happen. As the climate grew warmer, the large herds of animals that had roamed the land in earlier times slowly disappeared. There were fewer large animals, and the people found that hunting was no longer as easy. Their old way of life must have died out slowly. It is thought that this probably affected every part of their lives, because the cave art of Europe came to an end at about the same time.

The first farmers

As the Ice Age ended, important developments were taking place in what are now parts of Israel, Turkey and Iran. Wild grasses grew abundantly there, and people began to collect grass seeds for food. They got so much food from the grasses that they were able to live in one place and build villages – something that nobody had ever done before. In time, they realized that they could have even more food by planting the grass seeds for themselves. These people had become the first farmers.

They later learned to keep animals – such as goats – and grow crops. And as they continued growing food plants, they always selected the best seed to sow. In this way, the grasses they had begun with gradually improved, until they became the cereals (wheat, barley and rye) that we know today. In Central America, other people cultivated corn, and in Asia rice became the main cereal crop.

Early farmers used sickles made of sharp flints set in an animal's jawbone.

Domestic goats were bred from wild species.

Teosinte, wild grass of Central America | Modified teosinte | Further modification | Primitive corn | Modern corn

Jericho – the first city

The area where agriculture first began in the Near East is known as the Fertile Crescent, and it was there that the earliest cities were built. One of these cities – Jericho – has been discovered and excavated. Jericho is described in the Bible, but this was a later city, built on the ruins of the earlier one. Archaeologists have shown that the original Jericho was established about 9,500 years ago. It consisted of simple round huts, built of mud bricks. Around these huts the people built a huge wall. At one point there was a tower, used to keep a lookout over the countryside.

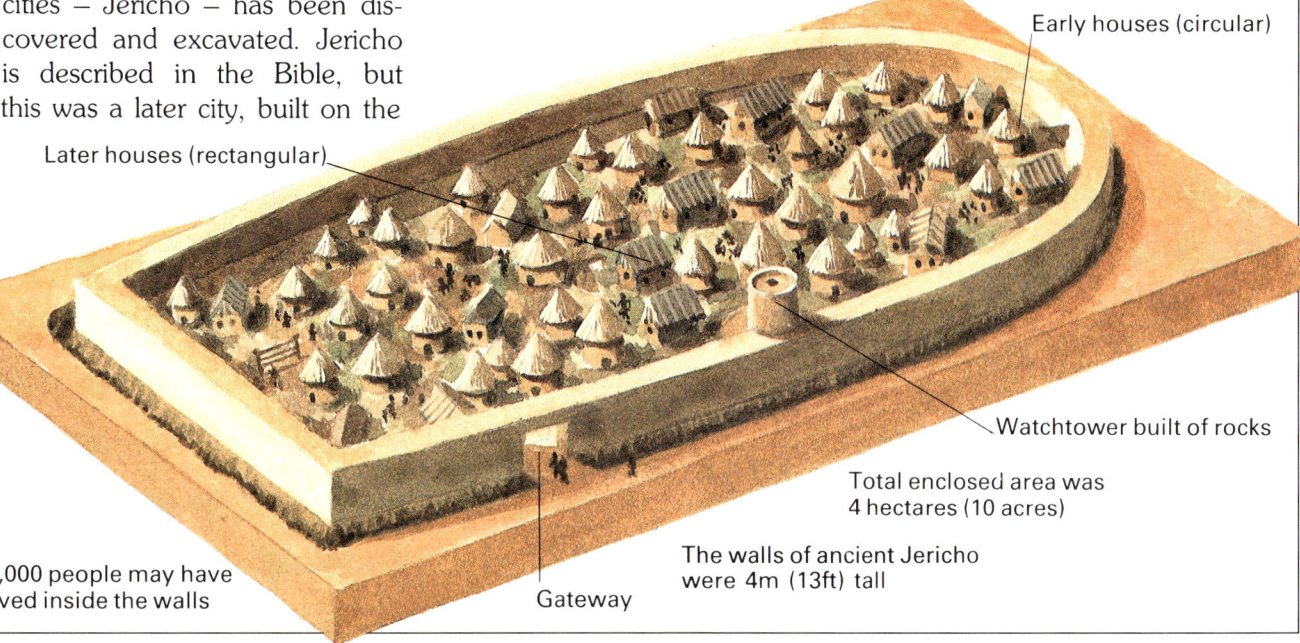

Early houses (circular)
Later houses (rectangular)
Watchtower built of rocks
Total enclosed area was 4 hectares (10 acres)
The walls of ancient Jericho were 4m (13ft) tall
2,000 people may have lived inside the walls
Gateway

Learning new skills

The earliest farmers had to store grain and other crops, just as farmers do today, to make sure they had enough food all year round. To protect this grain and their valuable herds of animals they were forced to defend themselves from nomadic raiders. The great walls of Jericho were built to keep them out.

The first farmers also needed containers to keep food and water in, and to cook their food in, because large amounts of cereals such as wheat cannot be eaten raw. At first they would have used baskets for storage, and animal skins sewn up into waterproof bags. But in time they developed a better type of container – pottery. Initially, they may have applied wet clay to a basket and dried it over a fire to make it waterproof. Later they learned to mold the clay into a container without using a basket as a base. Pottery was first made at Jericho about 8,000 years ago. It was invented independently by the Indians of Central America 4,000 years ago.

Pots are still made without using a potter's wheel.

17

THE RISE OF CIVILIZATION

Irrigation began at least 7,000 years ago in both the Near East and China, although on a fairly small scale. Larger scale irrigation systems are found in the Near East, in the area known as Mesopotamia, from about 5,000 years ago onward. The first city states began to emerge in Mesopotamia 6-5,000 years ago. Metal smelting was well developed by 5,000 years ago – the beginning of the Bronze Age. The Iron Age began about 3,000 years ago. Writing and the wheel were both invented 6-5,000 years ago.

The people of Jericho were probably members of a tribe, and they would have had a leader or leaders. But everyone was more or less equal, and no one was very wealthy. It is thought that these people may have worshipped their ancestors because they made the images of dead people by building up features of plaster and shell on their skulls. As time went by, religion became a more and more important part of the people's lives, and a group of priests or priestesses probably developed and became very powerful. This stage of development is seen at a city called Catal Huyuk in southern Turkey.

The next stage of development in the Near East is seen in the great city states of Mesopotamia such as Ur and Uruk. These were ruled by kings who were immensely powerful – when they died, hundreds of soldiers and court attendants were put to death and buried alongside them.

Cities and religion

Catal Huyuk shows how far society had developed 7,000 years ago. Its inhabitants still belonged to the Stone Age, because their tools were made from hard black stone called obsidian. But they lived in a large city of over 5,000 people and built special temples for worshipping their gods. Their religion centered on bulls and on a Great Goddess.

The people of Catal Huyuk left their dead out on platforms to be eaten by vultures. The bones were then brought in and buried in the houses, underneath the platforms on which the people slept.

To make them easier to defend, neither the houses nor the temples had doors – they were entered by ladders leading down from holes in the roof. The people walked from one house to another across the roofs.

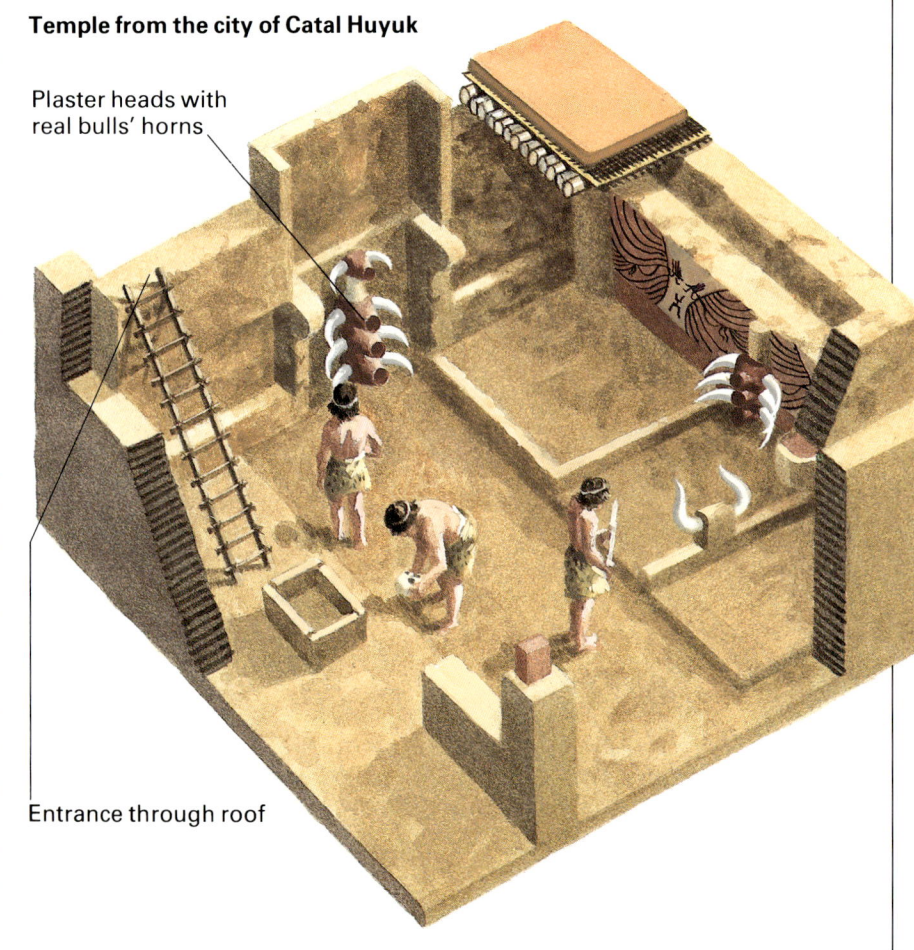

Temple from the city of Catal Huyuk

Plaster heads with real bulls' horns

Entrance through roof

From stone to metal

Stone had been used for tools for over two million years, and it was still used by the people of Jericho and Catal Huyuk. But they also discovered rocks containing the metal copper, and they began using it to make jewelry. This copper was in its pure form which is unusual – most copper, and almost all other metals, are found as ores, and they have to be heated (smelted) to get the metal itself out of the ore. By 5,000 years ago, people in the Near East had learned to smelt ores and they were beginning to make tools out of bronze – a mixture of copper and tin. Slowly the use of stone tools died out. Later it was found that another metal – iron – was harder than bronze and this was used instead.

Hittite metalwork dating from 2500 BC

The city states

The people of Catal Huyuk obviously lived well – archaeologists believe they controlled the trade in obsidian which allowed them to become wealthy. But there do not seem to have been any kings or other rulers who were much richer than others, and priestesses probably held power.

About 6,000 years ago, much larger cities began to develop which were ruled by royal families, who became very rich and powerful. These new city states, such as Ur and Uruk, were mostly in the river valleys, whereas Jericho and Catal Huyuk were in the foothills of mountains. Massive irrigation projects – bringing water to farmland by specially constructed channels – may have been important in the development of these new city states. Small-scale irrigation had been practiced in hilly areas, but in the river valleys it was possible on a larger scale, and this needed better organized societies. It was in these city states that important advances, such as writing, the building of larger ships and the invention of the wheel, were made.

A wheeled chariot of 2500 BC from Sumaria

EXPLORATION/COLONIZATION

If a hunter-gatherer band drifts about 20 km (12 miles) in a generation, then they could cover up to 14,000 km (8,700 miles) in 20,000 years. This is the distance from East Africa to Peking – a journey that was probably made by *Homo erectus* over 500,000 years ago.

The earliest people were hunter-gatherers and they lived a nomadic existence, wandering from place to place. They could have gradually wandered into new areas without making any deliberate effort to do so – and without even being aware that they were discovering new lands. In this way, *Homo erectus* and *Homo sapiens* conquered most of Europe and Asia, and *Homo sapiens sapiens* continued into North and South America, Australia, New Zealand and Polynesia. Exploration and colonization of new lands has continued to the present day.

The discovery of America

American Indian

During the ice ages there was a great deal of water 'locked up' in the ice caps at the north and south poles. Because of this, there was less water in the sea, and the sea level fell all around the world. Places that are now shallow seas were then dry land, including the Bering Strait that separates Asia from North America. Between about 30,000 and 10,000 years ago, bands of *Homo sapiens* from Asia wandered into this area, and continued southeastward – thus discovering North America. These people expanded into the unexplored continent, and had reached South America by at least 12,000 years ago. Because Amerindians are descended from Asian peoples they have Mongoloid features: little facial hair in men, and a fold of skin over the upper eyelid.

Some Eskimos still follow a traditional way of life.

Crossing the seas

Australia, New Zealand and Polynesia were colonized by people from Southeast Asia. Australian Aborigines probably arrived about 40,000 years ago, in canoes or on rafts. They brought domesticated dogs, which later returned to the wild – the dingoes. They remained as hunter-gatherers but boat building became a forgotten skill.

The people who discovered Polynesia made epic ocean voyages in their large, well-made canoes, which they still build today. Some held up to 100 people. During a period of great expansion they reached New Zealand and gave rise to the Maoris.

Polynesians in a sea-going canoe

European colonization

Although most of the world's peoples became farmers, they did not stop moving about and colonizing new areas. There was always a hunger for new lands because of population growth.

Once most areas had been settled, migration resulted in conflict between the existing populations and those newly arrived. A pattern of migration and conflict became common in most parts of the world, particularly in Europe and Asia, and this continued down the ages.

The most dramatic migration of any human group since prehistoric times was the movement out of Europe that began almost 300 years ago and is still continuing. The Spanish and Portuguese conquest of South America began in 1493 and was followed by the British and French settlement of North America, and the British colonization of Australia and New Zealand. At the same time, Portuguese, Dutch and British settlers claimed land in parts of Africa. Like earlier migrations, this European expansion has caused great conflict and heavy losses of life among native peoples of the areas colonized. Groups such as the Australian Aborigines, the Amerindians and the Maoris have lost much of their land and, in most cases, their traditional way of life.

Spanish soldiers besieged by Mexican Indians

Australian Aborigines demonstrate for land rights

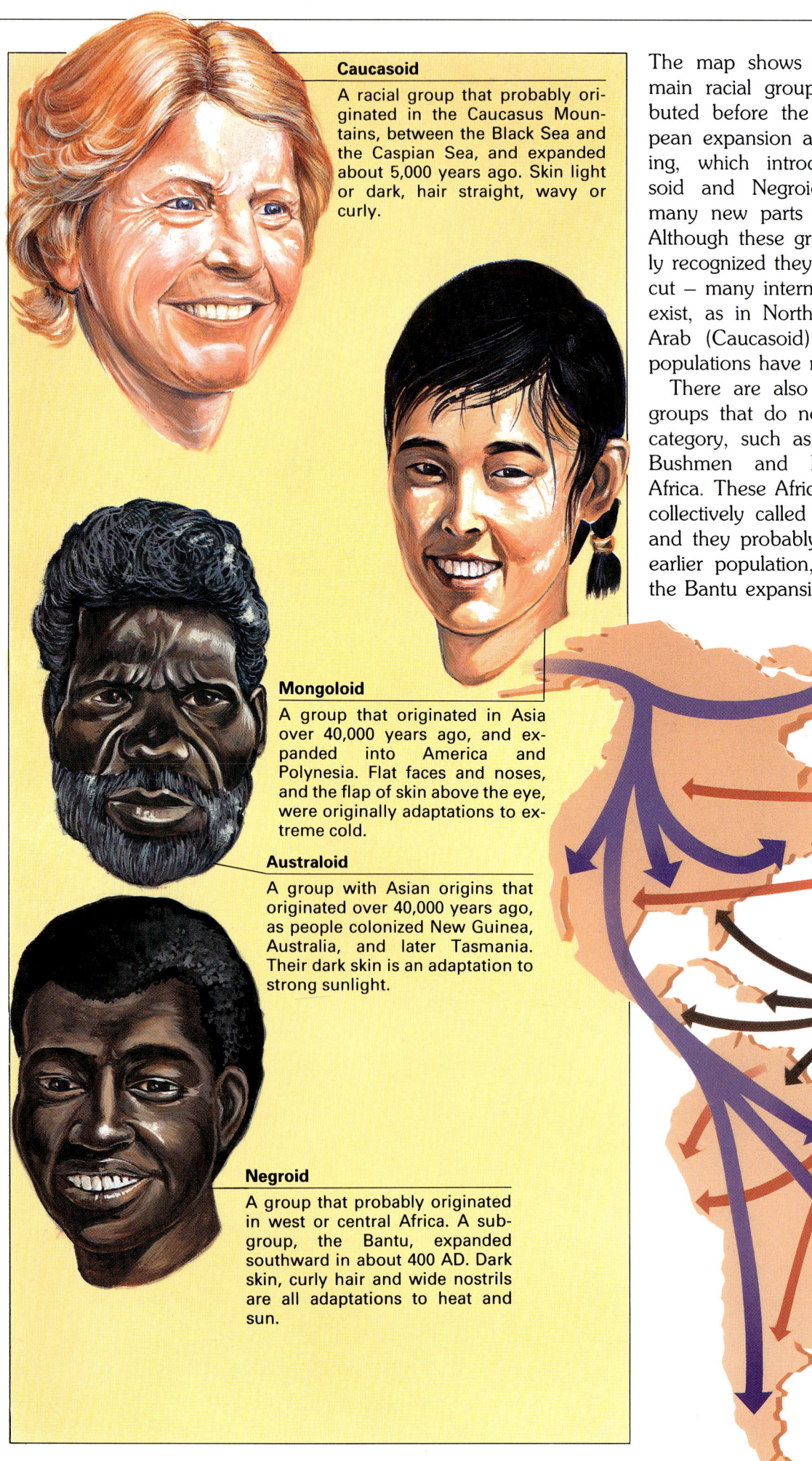

Caucasoid

A racial group that probably originated in the Caucasus Mountains, between the Black Sea and the Caspian Sea, and expanded about 5,000 years ago. Skin light or dark, hair straight, wavy or curly.

Mongoloid

A group that originated in Asia over 40,000 years ago, and expanded into America and Polynesia. Flat faces and noses, and the flap of skin above the eye, were originally adaptations to extreme cold.

Australoid

A group with Asian origins that originated over 40,000 years ago, as people colonized New Guinea, Australia, and later Tasmania. Their dark skin is an adaptation to strong sunlight.

Negroid

A group that probably originated in west or central Africa. A subgroup, the Bantu, expanded southward in about 400 AD. Dark skin, curly hair and wide nostrils are all adaptations to heat and sun.

The map shows how the four main racial groups were distributed before the era of European expansion and slave trading, which introduced Caucasoid and Negroid peoples to many new parts of the world. Although these groups are easily recognized they are not clear-cut — many intermediate groups exist, as in North Africa where Arab (Caucasoid) and Negroid populations have mixed.

There are also some smaller groups that do not fit into any category, such as the Pygmies, Bushmen and Hottentots of Africa. These African groups are collectively called the Khoisans, and they probably represent an earlier population, displaced by the Bantu expansion.

PEOPLES OF THE WORLD

As our early ancestors moved into new parts of the world, they had to adapt to different climatic conditions. In hot sunny climates, for example, dark skins are favored because they absorb some of the sun's harmful radiation. But as people moved into colder northern areas, dark skins became a disadvantage. The action of sunlight on skin helps us make vitamin D, an important substance that aids the growth of the bones: in cloudy conditions, dark skins absorb too little of the sunlight, which can cause vitamin D deficiency.

Where people moved south again – as when the Caucasoid peoples migrated into India – they developed dark skins once more. Adaptations to climate such as this produced different racial groups and subgroups in different parts of the world.

The races of mankind show no differences in intelligence. The same set of blood groups occurs in all races, although there are differences in the frequency of blood groups. Other comparisons at the molecular level confirm the evidence of the blood groups: there are no fundamental differences between the races.

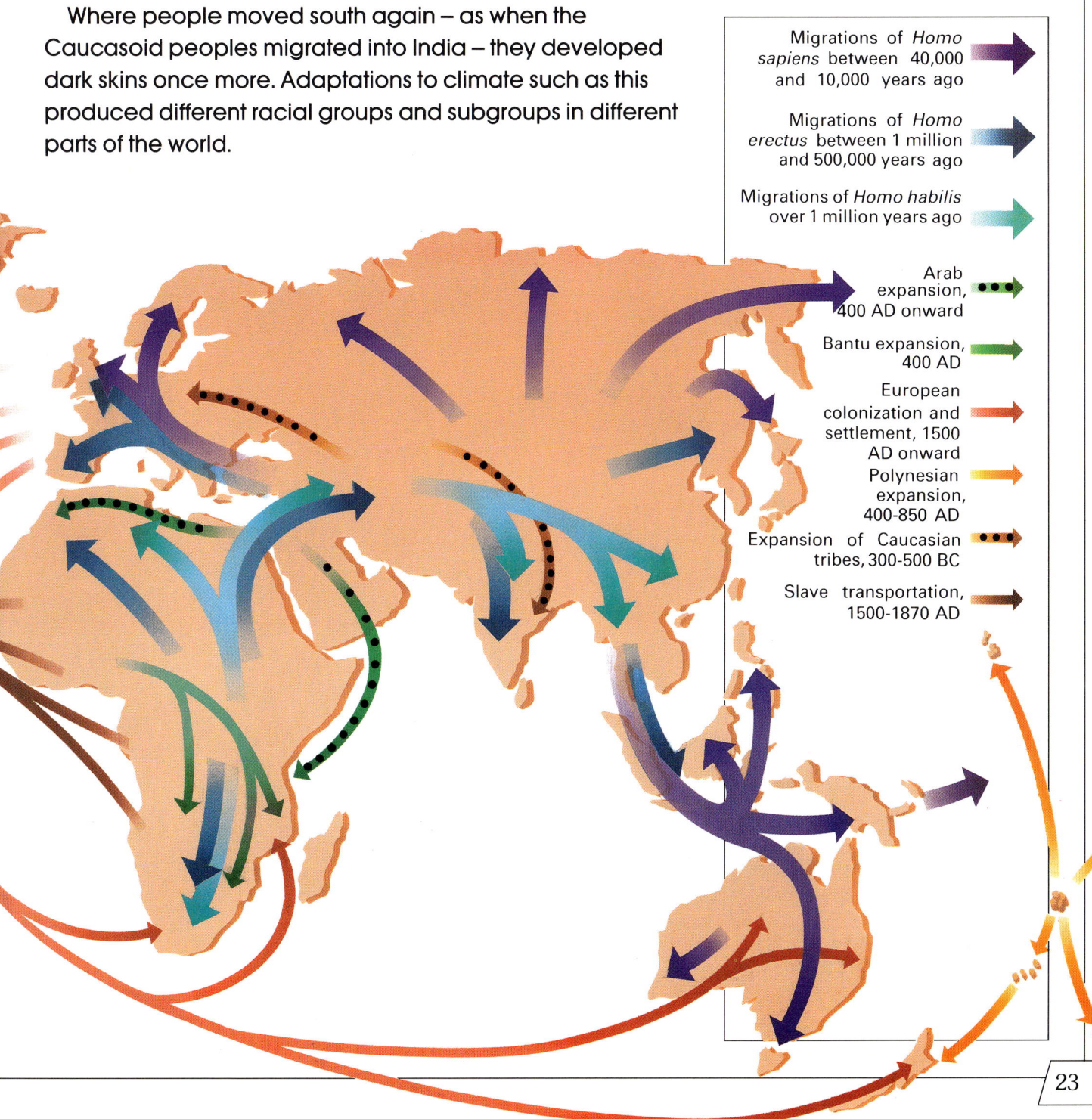

Migrations of *Homo sapiens* between 40,000 and 10,000 years ago

Migrations of *Homo erectus* between 1 million and 500,000 years ago

Migrations of *Homo habilis* over 1 million years ago

Arab expansion, 400 AD onward

Bantu expansion, 400 AD

European colonization and settlement, 1500 AD onward

Polynesian expansion, 400-850 AD

Expansion of Caucasian tribes, 300-500 BC

Slave transportation, 1500-1870 AD

HUMAN LANGUAGE

There are thousands of different languages spoken around the world, many of them used only by a small group of people. Of the major languages, English is the most widely used with over 700 million speakers. But English is the mother tongue for only half of these people – for the others it is a second language. In terms of native speakers, Mandarin Chinese is the most common language, with 600 million people using it as their mother tongue.

No one knows exactly when our ancestors first began to speak, but some clues come from looking at fossil skulls. Because the skull fits the brain like a glove, it can show what shape the brain was, and scientists can make some deductions about language use from the brain shape. It seems from ancient skulls that *Homo habilis* had already begun to develop a simple sort of language. In time, this language would have become more complex and structured, and fossil skulls show that in Neanderthals language was probably fully developed. As hominids migrated to new areas they would have begun to develop different languages. When groups are no longer in touch with each other, they begin to invent new words and use old words differently. Eventually they speak totally different languages.

Languages of the world

We tend to think that for each nation there is just one clearly-defined language – French in France, German in Germany and so on. In fact this is an unusual state of affairs, the result of deliberate policies by the nations of Europe over several centuries. To achieve a sense of national identity, governments have discouraged local dialects, and taught a standard version of the official language in schools.

The pattern of languages found in Africa is far more natural. Each small district speaks its own dialect, although this has many similarities to the dialects of neighboring regions. People from one district will understand those from nearby districts, but not those from further away. At one time, this language pattern would have been found all around the world.

The languages of the world can be grouped into families on the basis of their similarities. As the larger map shows, the distribution of language families often reflects ancient patterns of migration – the Indo-European languages correspond to the spread of Caucasoid peoples over 2,500 years ago. Official languages, on the other hand, tend to reflect more recent eras of conquest and settlement, particularly the period of European colonization.

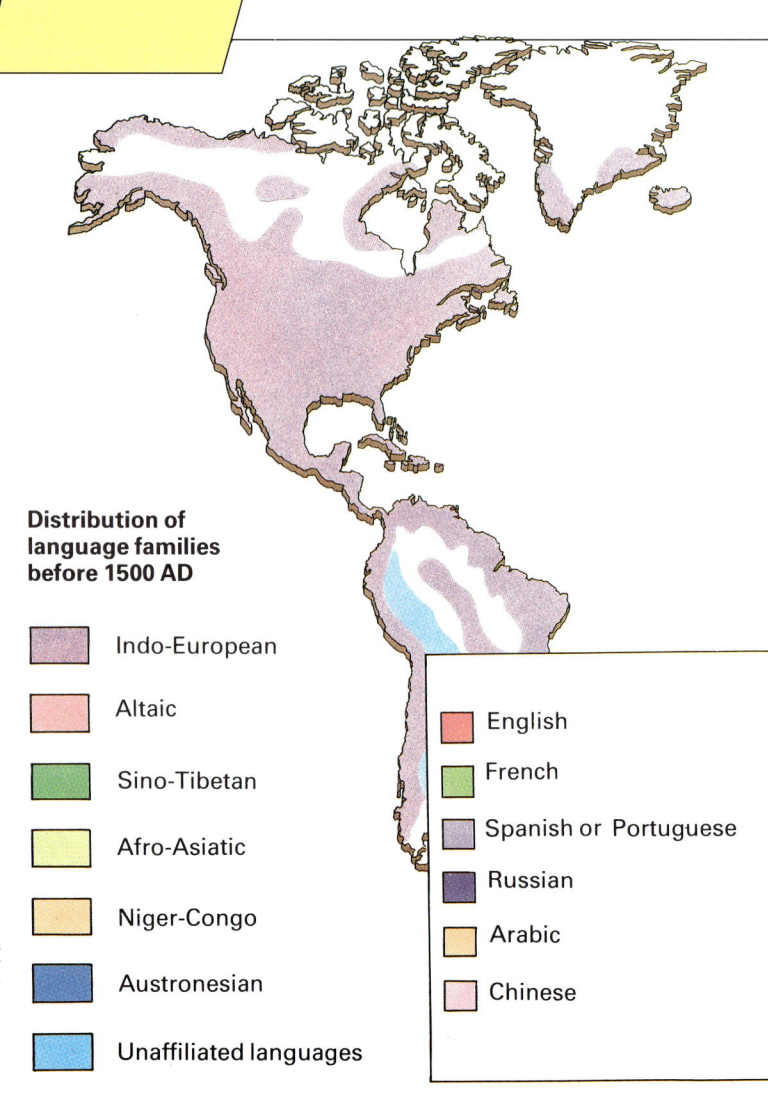

Distribution of language families before 1500 AD

- Indo-European
- Altaic
- Sino-Tibetan
- Afro-Asiatic
- Niger-Congo
- Austronesian
- Unaffiliated languages

- English
- French
- Spanish or Portuguese
- Russian
- Arabic
- Chinese

Teaching apes to 'talk'

Animals communicate with each other by sounds and movements but their "language" is very different from ours. Each call or display has a specific meaning such as "keep away, this is my territory" or "please give me some of that food." An animal cannot "say" anything original – all its messages are much the same as those of its parents and grandparents.

Chimpanzees are highly intelligent and there have been several attempts to teach them human language. They cannot actually learn to talk, because the shape of the mouth and throat is different, but they can be taught a sign language used by deaf people. They grasp the concept of naming – linking particular signs with particular objects. But they do not form sentences, a fundamental difference between their mental abilities and ours.

Chimpanzees can be taught sign language.

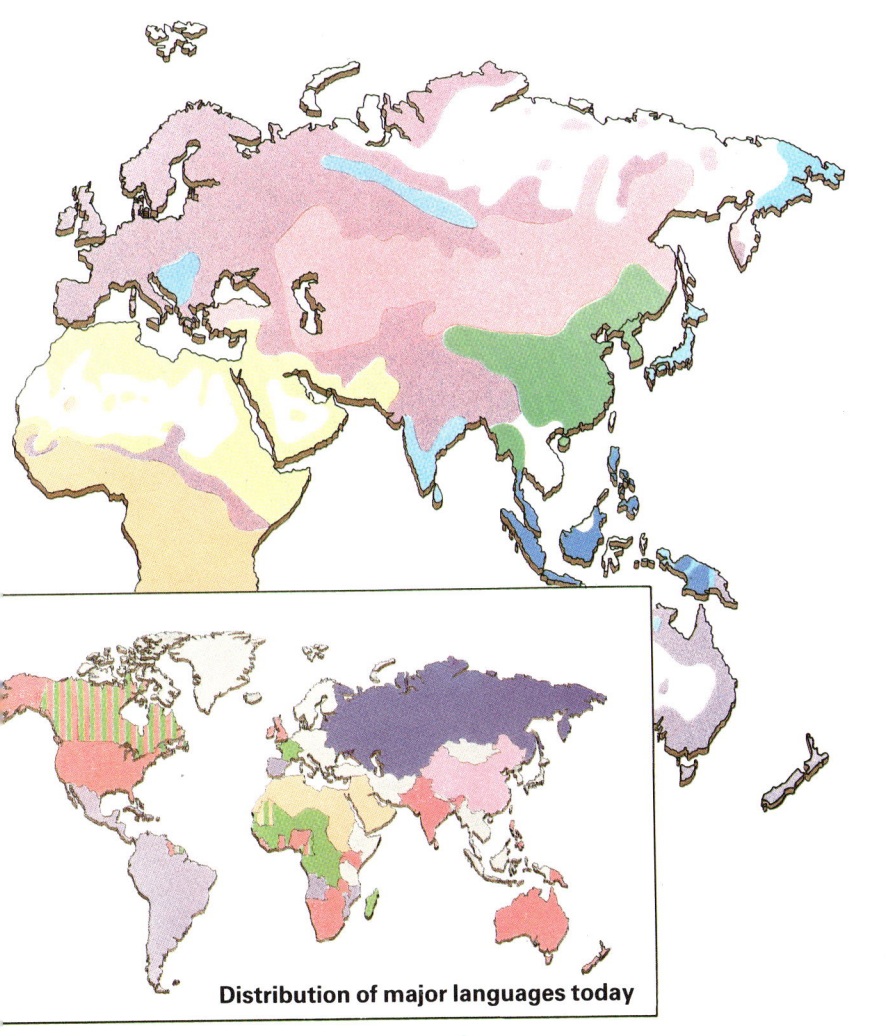
Distribution of major languages today

Non-verbal communication

Before our ancestors learned to talk they communicated by sounds and gestures. This type of non-verbal communication persists today, and is often called body language. We also have symbols that can be understood by anyone, regardless of what language they speak.

International symbols

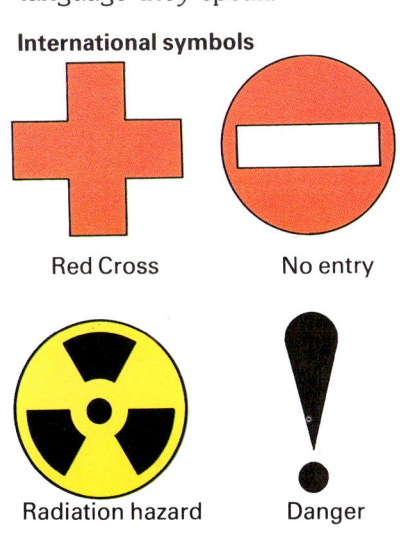

Red Cross No entry

Radiation hazard Danger

RELIGIONS AND CUSTOMS

There are over 1.3 billion Christians, 690 million Muslims, 450 million Hindus and 200 million Buddhists in the world today. A further 200 million people practice local religions with no written teachings, called "non-scriptural" religions.

Religions are common to all cultures, but they are enormously varied, and their beliefs and moral teachings often contradict each other. To the individual, religion is the recognition of a superhuman spiritual power to whom prayers are addressed, either formally in a place of worship or informally at home – individually or as a group. Formal worship takes place in the many splendid and historic churches, cathedrals, mosques and temples throughout the world, and there are many ceremonies and rituals such as christenings, marriages and funerals which are associated with each religion.

The major religions

There are thousands of different religions practiced around the world. As with languages, there are a few major religions, with millions of followers, and many local ones, practiced by only small groups of people. Local religions are often very complex and some involve a great many gods and goddesses, about whom many legends are told. Animal spirits or gods are common, and there is usually a story that explains how the world was made – a "creation myth." Myths and legends are also important in the major religions, but they are written down. Together with codes of conduct and other teachings, they form scriptures – the Bible for Christianity, the Old Testament and Talmud for Judaism, the Koran for Islam and the sacred Vedas for Hinduism.

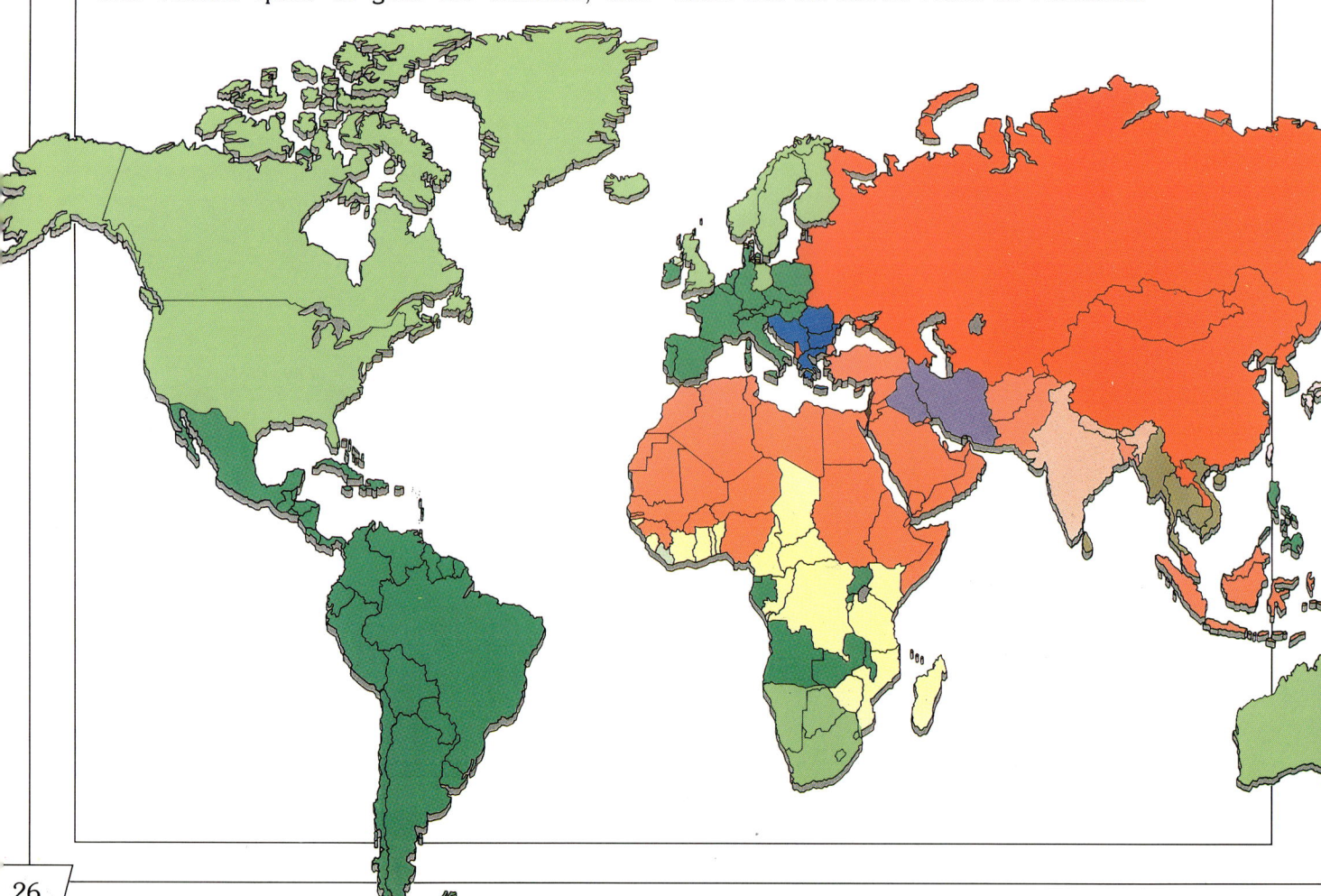

Rites of passage

Most religions have ceremonies for newborn babies, such as the Christian service of baptism. There are also funeral services following death in almost all religions. These ceremonies are known as rites of passage because they mark the passing of a person from one state to another. Rites of passage may also be celebrated at a particular time in a person's life, such as when he or she reaches puberty (sexual maturity), or the age of adulthood, as with the Bar Mitzvah ceremony for Jewish boys (performed at age 13). Marriage is another important rite of passage in many religions.

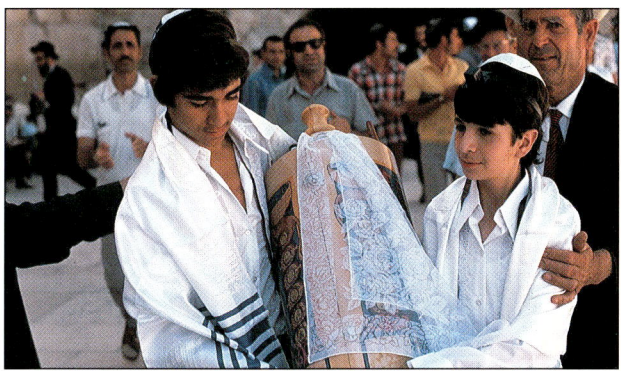

Jewish boys at their Bar Mitzvah

A wedding group poses for the camera in Kenya.

MAJOR RELIGIONS

- Roman Catholic ⎫
- Protestant ⎬ Christianity
- Greek or Russian Orthodox ⎭
- Sunni Muslims ⎫ Islam
- Shiite Muslims ⎭
- Hinduism
- Buddhism
- Shinto and other Japanese religions
- Judaism
- Communist states, in which people are officially atheist
- Non-scriptural religions

Religious wars

Religion has often been the cause of much hatred and conflict. Sometimes the dispute is over access to sacred sites — the fact that all the major religions had their origins in a fairly small area of Asia means that there are overlapping claims to some of the holy places. Jerusalem, for example, is a Holy City to Jews, Muslims and Christians. Often the conflict is not about sites, but results simply from intolerance of other religious groups, for example the occupation and forced eviction of the Sikhs in their sacred Golden Temple at Amritsar.

Armed Sikhs defending their Golden Temple

THE THIRD WORLD

> More than 500 million people in the Third World go hungry every day, and 40 million die from starvation, or diseases due to hunger, every year. Despite massive financial aid from the Western World, these problems will be likely to continue until these developing countries can build up their agriculture to feed their increasing populations.

There is no precise definition of the Third World, but it is usually employed to mean the underdeveloped countries of the world, including most African countries, Central and South America, India, Pakistan, China and much of southeastern Asia. Apart from China, most of these countries experienced European colonial rule. Some were part of the British Empire, others were ruled by France, Germany, Portugal or other European countries. South America was colonized by Spain and Portugal, but at a much earlier date.

The methods by which the colonial powers administered their colonies differed. Some like Britain preferred to rule indirectly with an administration that included people from the colonies themselves, while others such as Portugal ruled directly by establishing overseas states. In every case, however, the aim was to use the resources for the benefit of the colonial power.

Food and famine

In most colonies, the colonial power reorganized agriculture so that instead of growing food for themselves the people produced cash crops needed by the ruling country: coffee, tea, sugar, sisal (for rope and sacks), rubber, bananas or pineapples. The colony could use the cash it earned to buy the food and machinery it needed from the ruling country. The trading arrangements set up in the colonial era worked in the ruling countries' favor because they were economically stronger and could fix the prices of the cash crops produced by the colonies. The prices were always low, even after the colonies achieved independence, because the industrialized countries still had the upper hand economically. The former colonies did not have the resources to restructure their agriculture and return to producing all their own food.

Workers picking tea in Darjeeling, India

A sugar cane plantation in Barbados

Political problems

As the developing countries gained their independence they were left with political and economic problems. There had been many changes during colonization, and much of their income from the cash crops was still controlled by the former colonial powers. The new governments also had little experience of ruling.

Often there were several political factions striving for power, and this caused the frequent overthrows of governments. Due to this most developing countries have a strong central government, run by a single political party. Colonization also left a legacy of new boundaries and the settlement of people from one part of the world to another. Under British rule, for example, Tamils were taken from India to work on the plantations in Sri Lanka. Today these developing countries are generally more stable, but there are still examples of internal strife and guerrilla war in places like Ethiopia, Chad, Angola and Sri Lanka.

Tamil freedom-fighters in Sri Lanka

The population crisis

Population growth in developed countries is now small because contraception is widely used. But in most developing countries, where there is no "welfare state," people need to have large families to ensure that there is somebody to look after them in their old age. Because many children die of infectious diseases, parents have large families to make sure that some will survive. Only when life becomes more secure do people voluntarily limit the size of their families.

Even if some economic growth does take place, the economies of the developing countries cannot support the rise in population and many people go hungry. Many drift to the towns, where they live in vast makeshift shanty towns around the large cities. These areas lack basic amenities such as clean water and sanitation, and there is no full-time work for most of the inhabitants. As living conditions improve the death and infant mortality rates are bound to fall, thus accelerating the population growth and increasing the unemployment problems. Governments can organize family planning campaigns, but this may run up against social and religious barriers.

A shanty town at the edge of Rio, Brazil

THE INDUSTRIAL AGE

Before the 18th century, over 80 per cent of the population worked on the land. Today the figure in the United States is 2 per cent of a much larger total population. Using highly mechanized methods, these few farmers feed the entire American population and produce food for export. The Industrial Revolution was marked by the invention of new machines such as the spinning jenny. This led to the creation of new industries and new factory systems.

The earliest people were hunter-gatherers: they ate foods collected from the wild. There are still nomadic people who live by hunting and gathering, but with the invention of agriculture most people became farmers. They settled in more permanent villages and as the food production rose, so they were able to support themselves in greater numbers. The human population began to grow – as did the numbers of villages and communities surrounding the agricultural areas. Those not working directly in agriculture were involved in associated industries which began to flourish – for example, blacksmiths made tools and handled the shoeing of horses. The change in the way people lived was called the Agricultural Revolution.

During the late 18th Century the Industrial Revolution started in Britain, and quickly followed in Europe, North America and Australasia.

The Industrial Revolution

The Industrial Revolution began with the invention of farm machinery that could do much of the heavy work formerly done by laborers or horses. These machines were powered by steam engines which burned coal – in effect, coal power was replacing muscle power. With fewer workers needed on the land, many people drifted to the towns where newly built factories employed them in manufacturing. But there was enormous hardship because working conditions were poor, wages were low and working hours were long. New housing areas that had been built to accomodate the influx of people into the cities became slums. Only when the rights of the workers became recognized through the establishment of trade unions did workers' conditions improve.

Today an industrialized society exists throughout the Western world, including Japan. Factory workers can expect a high level of safety and good working conditions. Trade unions representing the workers are well organized and negotiate on their behalf with the management.

Women working in a nineteenth-century factory

Some industrial housing developed into slums.

The nuclear family

The increasing tendency for people in the Western World to move around in search of better-paying jobs has led to a new way of life for the family. In the past the "extended family" consisted of parents and children living with or near grandparents and other relatives. The whole group helped raise the children and also supported the elderly through sickness and death. Today's "nuclear family" typically consists of parents and their one to three children, often living great distances from other relatives. The lack of extended support has often caused hardship, to old and young alike. Care for elderly relatives may have to be provided in old people's homes. And the growing tendency for both parents to be at work means that the children have to be left under supervision during the day.

Parents and children – a Western nuclear family

Farming as technology

In farming, industrialization has continued at the same pace up to the present day, with newer and larger machines continually replacing the earlier ones. At the same time, more and more chemicals have been used: artificial fertilizers to increase crop yields, pesticides to kill fungi and insect pests, and herbicides to kill weeds. The result of this modernization is that far more food can be produced from the same area of land using fewer workers.

Associated with agriculture are many industries that are involved in the food production process. Fertilizers, pesticides, processing, packaging and transport may all be required before the product reaches the marketplace.

The illustration on the right shows the various costs that are included in the price of a loaf of bread.

Combine harvesters cutting wheat

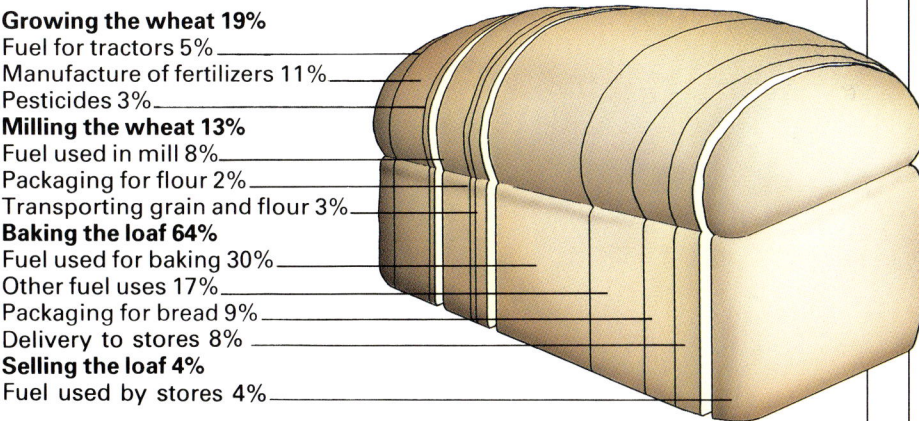

Growing the wheat 19%
Fuel for tractors 5%
Manufacture of fertilizers 11%
Pesticides 3%
Milling the wheat 13%
Fuel used in mill 8%
Packaging for flour 2%
Transporting grain and flour 3%
Baking the loaf 64%
Fuel used for baking 30%
Other fuel uses 17%
Packaging for bread 9%
Delivery to stores 8%
Selling the loaf 4%
Fuel used by stores 4%

THE HIGH-TECH AGE

There are 300 communications satellites orbiting the Earth. One undersea telephone cable can carry 5,000 telephone calls. There are now enough nuclear weapons to destroy the entire world population twenty times over; $1.5 million are spent on arms every minute.

Technology began 2 million years ago with the making of the first stone tools. It progressed slowly over hundreds of thousands of years, but with the start of the Industrial Revolution in the 18th century, rapid changes occurred. Today we can build computers that can "think," make robots that assemble cars and "design" bacteria to produce medical drugs. We can send men into space and bounce messages around the world by satellite. We can even harness the energy locked inside atoms to generate electricity – or possibly to destroy the planet on which we live

High-tech medicine

In medicine, new technology has brought enormous benefits. Body scanners, transplant surgery and other modern techniques mean that many people who would once have died are still alive. But the cost of high-tech medicine is enormous, and the problem of how to finance it has to be tackled by all societies.

The contrast with health provision in the Third World is striking. While we may spend thousands of dollars keeping one person alive, millions of children in Africa and Asia die for want of vaccines that cost only a few cents. Often the high-tech treatments, such as heart operations, are used to cure self-inflicted conditions produced by smoking or overeating.

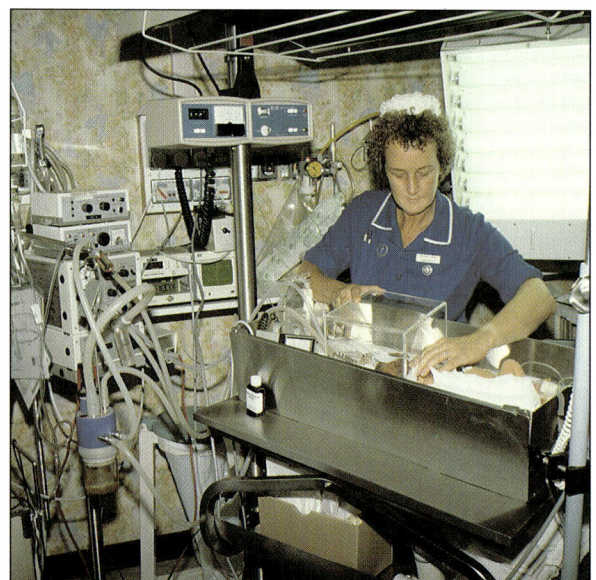

Babies benefit from high-tech medicine.

The power in a nucleus

Nuclear power and nuclear weapons are based on the same principle: if certain atoms are split, huge amounts of energy are released. It took scientists many decades to learn to split atoms in a controlled way, and the first use of this new technology was in the atomic bombs dropped on Hiroshima and Nagasaki in Japan at the end of World War II. Since then, nine countries have developed nuclear weapons, and many more have harnessed nuclear power to generate electricity.

Splitting atoms produces radioactive materials, which are dangerous to all living things. They kill by damaging the cells that make up our bodies.

Nuclear missiles pose a threat to world peace.

The global village

Five million years ago the human race had its origins on the open plains of Africa. For many centuries this early hominid group must have formed a single community, until it got bigger and began to migrate outward and occupy new areas. That process of migration eventually led human beings to the most distant parts of the Earth. In the process it produced the many different races, cultures, languages and religions that we see today.

One of the achievements of the 20th century has been to put human beings from all parts of the world in touch with each other again. A telephone call can reach somebody on the other side of the planet. Today's jumbo and supersonic airliners transport millions of passengers from continent to continent and the journey takes only a few hours. Satellites send live television pictures from one continent to another. News programs bring the reality of war and famine in distant lands into our own homes. In effect we are again part of a single worldwide community – a vast global village – as early humans were five million years ago.

Modern travel has brought people closer together.

Television has made one world smaller; a dish aerial receives satellite pictures from another continent.

HUMAN EVOLUTIONARY TREE

This evolutionary tree is based on two types of evidence: fossil and molecular. The part dealing with the hominids is based on fossils, and some intelligent guesswork for the period before 1.5 million years ago.

There are few fossil-bearing rocks in Africa for the period between 10-4 million years ago. The date for the ape-human split and the relationships between the apes have therefore been worked out from molecular evidence. The main molecules used are proteins, which play an important role in the body as enzymes.

Enzymes control biochemical reactions, and certain parts of an enzyme molecule are crucial to how they work. But other parts are not and these non-essential parts can gradually change over the centuries.

Once two species separate, the non-essential parts of their enzyme molecules begin to change in different ways. The more differences there are, the longer the species have been separated.

Apes:
1 Gibbons and siamangs *Hylobates*
2 Orangutan *Pongo pygmaeus*
3 Gorilla *Gorilla gorilla*
4 Pygmy chimpanzee *Pan paniscus*
5 Chimpanzee *Pan troglodytes*

Hominids:
6 "Lucy" *Australopithecus afarensis*
7 Gracile australopithecine *Australopithecus africanus*
8 "Handyman" *Homo habilis*
9 Robust australopithecine (South African) *Australopithecus robustus*
10 Robust australopithecine (East African) *Australopithecus boisei*
11 *Homo erectus*
12 Neanderthal *Homo sapiens neanderthalensis*
13 Fully modern man *Homo sapiens sapiens*

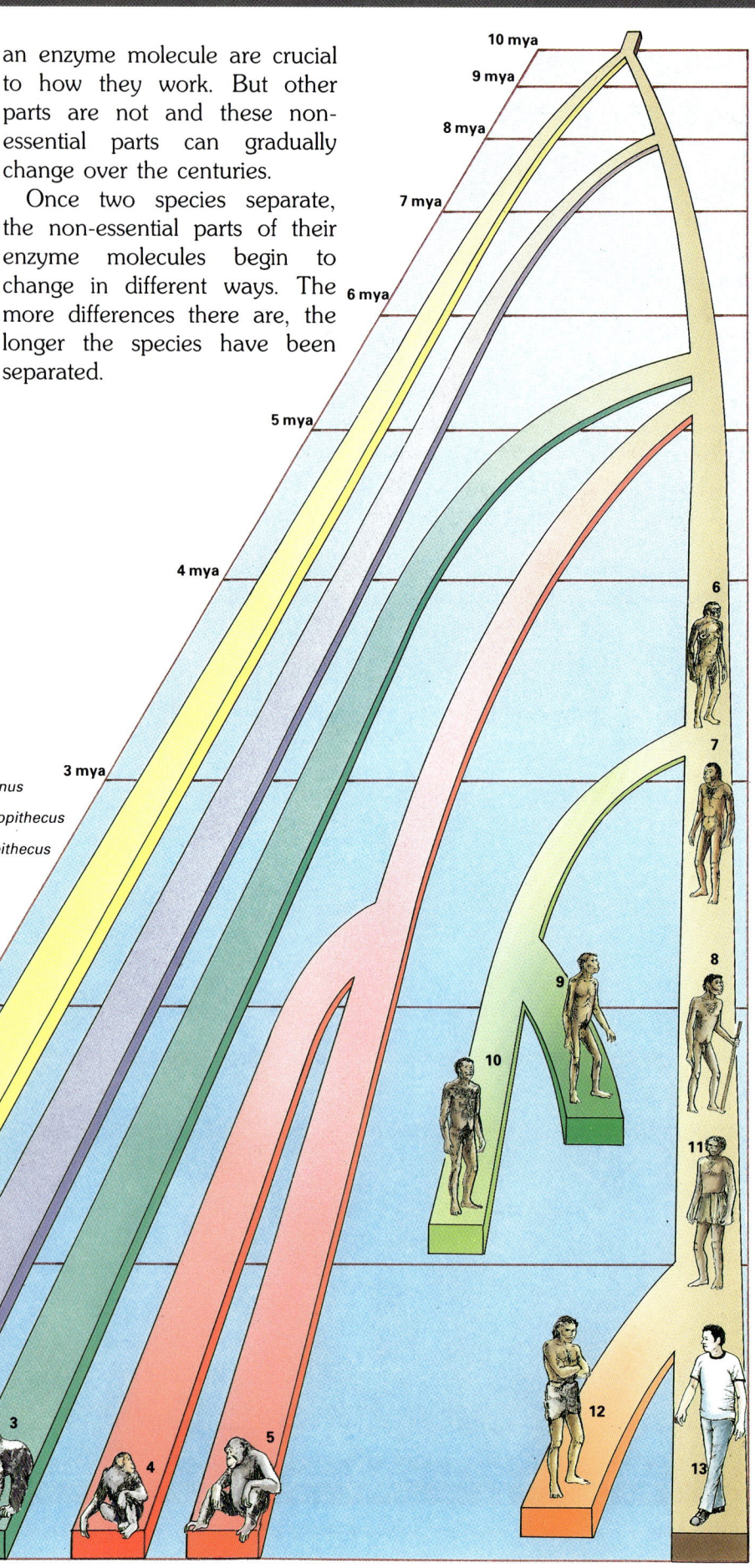

mya = million years ago

GLOSSARY

archaeology the study of evidence about the past found buried in the ground, particularly things that people have made or built, such as glass, pottery, stone tools, houses, ships and cities.

australopithecine an early human-like creature that walked upright but still had a fairly small brain, like that of an ape.

blood group the type of blood that a person has. Blood group is determined by the types of proteins found in the blood. There are four main blood groups: O, A, B and AB.

DNA the genetic material that carries all the information needed to make a living organism. It also controls the living processes of organisms.

electron microscope an instrument used for looking at extremely small objects. Instead of using light to "see," it uses a beam of electrons – some of the smallest particles known to man. Because the electrons are so small they allow us to "see" objects that are themselves very tiny.

evolution the process whereby living creatures gradually change from one generation to the next, becoming better suited to their environment in the process.

fossil a replica of a living organism, made in rock by natural processes, following the burial of the organism under a layer of silt or sand.

fossil fuels coal, oil and natural gas: fuels that have been formed, millions of years ago, from the dead bodies of plants or animals.

hominid any creature that is more human-like than ape-like. It includes the australopithecines as well as our direct ancestors.

hunter-gatherer a person who lives by hunting animals and collecting wild plants, nuts and berries for food. Until farming was invented, about 10,000 years ago, all humans were hunters-gatherers. There are still some people, mainly found in Africa, South America and Southeast Asia, who obtain their food in this way.

ice age a period when the earth's climate was much colder and the ice caps at the north pole stretched much further south. There were several ice ages, one after another, separated by warmer periods known as inter-glacials.

inorganic fertilizer substances used by farmers to make their crops grow bigger and produce a larger harvest. These fertilizers are made in factories and are applied to the fields as granules or dissolved in water. When it rains, they are easily washed away into streams and rivers, and may be harmful.

irrigation bringing water into a dry area, and directing and controlling the flow of water to help grow crops.

molecules the basic units of which all things are made up. Thus water is made up of water molecules, and chalk is made up of molecules of calcium carbonate. Living things are much more complex – they are made up of millions of different types of molecules.

nomadic wandering about from place to place instead of having a permanent home.

ore a special type of rock from which metal can be obtained.

paleontology the study of fossils.

pesticides substances that kill pests. They include insecticides, which kill insects, herbicides, which kill weeds, and fungicides, which kill fungi.

pottery a hard substance made by forming wet clay into the shape that is wanted and then baking it at very high temperatures. Typical uses of pottery today are in plates, and teacups.

prehistory the period before people began to record events in writing.

primate a mammal with forward-pointing eyes, a large brain, and hands that can grasp small or large objects. They include the monkeys, apes and humans.

proteins molecules that make up a large part of all living things. Proteins make our muscles contract, hold different parts of the body together and carry oxygen around. As enzymes, they also control all the chemical reactions taking place inside the body.

radioactivity high-energy rays that cannot be seen, but which can do great damage to living things. Many naturally occurring rocks and minerals are radioactive, and there is radioacivity in the world around us all the time. However, man-made radioactivity, particularly that produced by nuclear weapons and nuclear power-stations, adds to this background level.

species a groups of living creatures that all look the same or belong to a few recognizable types (male and female, for example, or workers and queens in the case of bees). All members of a species can breed with one another, but not with other plants or animals.

stone age a period of the past when our ancestors made tools out of stone.

technology making tools and machines to solve practical problems.

INDEX

All entries in bold are found in the Glossary

Aborigines 21
Afar Triangle 6
Africa 6-7, 8, 9, 10-11, 12, 14, 20-21, 24, 30, 31, 33
Agricultural Revolution 28
agriculture 16-17, 19, 21, 28-29, 30
apes 4, 6-7, 25, 34
Arab people 22, 23
archaeology 4, 8-9, 17, 19, **35**
art 4, 14-15, 16
Asia 11, 12, 20-21, 22
Australia 20-21, 22
Australoid people 22
australopithecines 7, 11, **35**
Australopithecus afarensis, see australopithecines

Bantu people 22, 23
Bering Strait 20
bones 4, 6-7, 9-10, 12-13, 15
brain size 7, 8, 10-12, 24
Britain 21, 30, 31
Bronze Age 18-19
brow-ridges 10, 12
burial customs 15
Bushmen 22

cash crops 30-31
Catal Huyuk 18-19
Caucasoid people 22, 23, 24
cave paintings 4, 13, 14-16
Central America 16-17, 21, 22, 30
cereals and grains 16
ceremonies and rituals 15, 26-27
China 11, 12, 16, 18, 20, 30
cities and villages 16-19, 28
city states 18, 19
climate 23
clothing 13
colonization 20-21, 22, 30-31, 33
communications 32-33
cooperation 8, 10
copper 19

customs 3, 26-27

dialects 24-25
diet and food 7, 10-11, 13, 14-15, 16-17, 28-29
domesticated animals 16, 21

Eskimos 12, 20
Ethiopia 6, 8
Europe 11, 12-13, 14, 16, 20-21, 22, 23
evidence 4-5, 8, 34
evolution 6-13, 34, **35**
extended family 29

farmers 16-17, 28-29
Fertile Crescent 17
fire 5, 10
flakes 8, 11
flint 9
footprints 4, 7
fossils 4, 6-7, 8, 12, 24, 26, 34, **35**
France 11, 13, 21, 30

gene pool 11

hammerstone 8
hand-axe 9, 10-11
hominids 6-11, 24, 33, **35**
Homo erectus 10-12, 20, 23
Homo habilis 8-9, 10-11, 12, 23, 24
Homo sapiens 12-13, 20, 23
Homo sapiens neanderthalensis, see Neanderthals
Homo sapiens sapiens 12-13, 20
Hottentots 22
hunter-gatherers 16, 20-21, 28, **35**
hunting 8-9, 10, 12, 16

Ice Age 12-13, 16, 20, **35**
India 30, 31
Indo-European languages 24
Industrial Revolution 28, 32

industrialization 28-33
intelligence 8, 10, 12, 23
Iran 16
Iron Age 18-19
irrigation 18-19, **35**
Italy 13

Japan 28, 32
Jericho 17, 18, 19

Kenya 10
Khoisans 22

La Marche cave 13, 14
language 8, 24-25, 33
lava 9
Lucy 6-7

magic 14, 15
mammoths 13
Maoris 21
medicine 32
Mesopotamia 18
metal smelting 18-19
metal tools 4, 19
Mexico 21
migrations 11, 13, 20-21, 22-23, 24, 33
modern man 11, 12-13
molecular evidence 6, 34
Mongoloid races 12, 20, 22, 23
myths 26

Neanderthals 12-13, 24, 26
Near East 16-19
Negroid people 22, 23
New Zealand 20-21
nomadic peoples 13, 17, 20-21, 28
North America 8, 20, 22
nuclear family 29
nuclear weapons 32

obsidian 18-19
Olorgessaillie 10
Omo Valley 8

Pakistan 11, 30
paleontology 4, 8, 12, **35**
Polynesia 20-21, 22, 23

population growth 21, 28, 31
Portugal 21, 30
pottery 4, 17, **35**
Pygmies 22

racial groups 3, 22-23, 33
raiders 17, 18
reindeer 13, 15
religion 15, 18, 26-27, 33
rulers 18, 19

Scandinavia 13
scavengers 9, 10
shamans 14, 15
shelter and houses 4, 12, 14-15, 17, 18, 28
ships 19, 21
Sikhs 27
skin color 23
skulls 8, 9, 10, 12, 18, 24
slave trade 22, 23
South Africa 31
South America 14, 20-21, 22, 30
Southeast Asia 16, 21, 30
Spain 11, 13, 21, 30
Sri Lanka 31
Stone Age 8-13, 18, **35**
stone tools 4, 7, 8-9, 10-11, 13, 18-19

Tamils 31
Tanzania 7, 14, 30
teeth 4, 7, 10, 12
Third World 30-32
tin 19
toe-bones 6-7
tools 4, 5, 7, 8-9, 10-11, 13, 14, 16, 18-19
tree-climbing 6, 7
tribal societies 10, 14, 18
Turkey 16, 18-19

Ur 18-19
Uruk 18-19

wheel 18, 19
writing 4, 18, 19, 26

Photographic Credits
Cover and pages 17, 21 (top), 28 (top), 32 (right) and back cover: Hutchison Library; contents page and page 9: Peter Kain; page 7: Mrs Jo Bond; pages 11, 16, 20, 29 (bottom) and 31 (bottom): Bruce Coleman; pages 13, 21 (left), 27 (left and top), 28 (bottom), 31 (top), 32 (left) and 33 (bottom inset): Robert Harding; pages 15 and 19 (top and bottom): Michael Holford; pages 21 (right), 27 (bottom), 29 (top) and 33 (bottom): Frank Spooner Agency; page 25: Ardea; page 30 (left and right): Mary Evans Library; page 33 (top): Lufthansa.